DORDOGNE TRAVEL GUIDE

The Updated Guide to the Best Attractions, Things to Do, Where to Stay, Food, and Culture of France's Gem Everything You Must Know Before Planning Your Trip to Dordogne

ANTHONY TURNER

Copyright © 2023 by Anthony Turner

All rights reserved. No part of this publication may be reproduced, distributed, or transmitted in any form or by any means, including photocopying, recording, or other electronic or mechanical methods, without the prior written permission of the publisher.

TABLE OF CONTENT

INTRODUCTION..5
    Why Visit the Dordogne?...8
    History and Culture Overview.. 11

CHAPTER 1:
PLANNING YOUR TRIP TO DORDOGNE............ 14
    When to Visit Dordogne... 18
    How to Get to Dordogne.. 20
    Getting Around in Dordogne... 22
    Where to Stay in Dordogne.. 25
    Choosing the Right Accommodation in Dordogne........28
    Must-Visit Restaurants and Foods to Try...................... 31
    Must-Try Tour Activities in Dordogne..........................34
    What to Pack for Your Trip to Dordogne...................... 37
    Entry and Visa Requirements..40
    Currency and Language... 43
    Suggested Budget... 45
    Money-Saving Tips..48
    Best Places to Book Your Trip.. 51

CHAPTER 2:
EXPLORING THE MEDIEVAL VILLAGES............ 54
    Sarlat-la-Canéda: A Journey Through Time..................56

    Beynac-et-Cazenac: Where History Comes Alive..........58

    Domme: Perched High Above the Dordogne................ 60

CHAPTER 3:
MAJESTIC CHÂTEAUX.. 63
    Château de Castelnaud: A Legendary Fortress..............65

    The Château de Beynac: A Medieval Wonder................67

    Château de Hautefort: Where Elegance Reigns............ 69

CHAPTER 4:
PREHISTORIC WONDERS................................... 71
    The Vézère Valley: A Gateway to the Past.....................73

    Lascaux: Unravel the Mysteries of Cave Art.................. 75

    Font-de-Gaume: A Glimpse into Ancient Life............... 77

    Rouffignac: Exploring the Cave of the Hundred Mammoths...79

CHAPTER 5:
OUTDOOR ADVENTURES.................................... 81
    Canoeing the Dordogne: A Serene River Escape...........83

    Hiking the Périgord Noir: Trails of Natural Beauty...... 85

Hot Air Balloon Rides: A Bird's-Eye View of the Valley 87

CHAPTER 6:
GASTRONOMY OF THE DORDOGNE................89

Truffles: The Black Gold of the Region......................... 91

Foie Gras: A Delicacy to Savor....................................... 93

Bergerac and Bordeaux Wines: Toasting to Excellence 95

CHAPTER 7:
IMMERSION IN LOCAL CULTURE......................97

Vibrant Markets: A Feast for the Senses....................... 99

Traditional Festivals: Celebrating Heritage and Tradition..101

Art and Craftsmanship: Discovering Local Talents..... 103

CHAPTER 8:
7-DAY ITINERARY IN DORDOGNE................... 105

Day 1: Arrival and Exploring Sarlat-la-Canéda............105

Day 2: Exploring Beynac-et-Cazenac and the Dordogne River...107

Day 3: Discovering the Prehistoric Wonders of the Vézère Valley..109

Day 4: Immersing in Natural Beauty - Gardens and Grotto Exploration...111

Day 5: Visiting Historic Towns and Villages................ 113

Day 6: Prehistoric Treasures and Local Delights......... 115

Day 7: Farewell to Dordogne..117

CHAPTER 9: PRACTICAL INFORMATION AND TIPS.. 119

Etiquette and Customs...119

Language and Communication.................................... 122

Simple French Phrases to Know...............................125

Health and Safety Tips... 128

Emergency Contacts..131

Communication and Internet Access.......................... 133

Useful Apps, Websites, and Maps................................ 136

CONCLUSION...139

INTRODUCTION

The Dordogne region is dear to my heart because it provided me with one of the most fascinating and unforgettable experiences of my life. I was enchanted by its timeless beauty, rich history, and the warmth of its people from the moment I arrived.

As I traveled through the area, I became enveloped in a tapestry of magnificent vistas that appeared to have erupted from the pages of a fairytale. The rolling hills, dotted with vineyards and sunflower fields, evoked a sense of pastoral tranquility.

The medieval settlements were like stepping back in time. Sarlat-la-Canéda took me back to the medieval age with its winding cobblestone lanes and immaculately preserved architecture. The aroma of freshly made pastries and the cheery conversation of people in bustling cafés produced a vibrant yet quiet ambiance.

Beynac-et-Cazenac, on the other hand, took a piece of my heart. Its cliffside castle towered magnificently over the settlement and the flowing river below. I was taken aback by the magnificent views from the castle's ramparts as I imagined the myriad stories that had occurred within those ancient walls.

The discovery of prehistoric beauties concealed beneath the Vézère Valley, however, was the highlight of my journey. I was amazed at the magnificent cave paintings depicting our ancestors' lives while visiting the renowned Lascaux cave.

Further into the valley, I visited Font-de-Gaume and Rouffignac, where the cave walls revealed additional historical secrets. I stared in amazement at the massive drawings that seemed to come to life under the flickering light in the dimly lit chambers.

Of course, my trip to the Dordogne included more than just history and natural splendor. The region's cuisine made an unforgettable impression on my taste buds. It was a gastronomic adventure unlike any other, indulging in the earthy flavors of truffles, savoring the velvety richness of foie gras, and matching it with the superb wines of Bergerac and Bordeaux. Each course seemed like a celebration of the region's culinary tradition and a testament to the chefs' devotion.

As my time in the Dordogne came to an end, I couldn't help but think about how welcoming the inhabitants were. I felt enveloped by the true warmth of the Dordogne community, whether it was engaging in friendly talks at the colorful markets or seeing the happy festivities of traditional festivals.

It was difficult to leave this magnificent place, but the memories of my stay in Dordogne remained with me, forever carved in my heart. The Dordogne gave me an experience that awoke my senses, expanded my comprehension of history, and sparked a deep respect for the beauty of life's basic pleasures.

I heartily recommend the Dordogne as a location that combines natural splendor, historical history, and unforgettable gastronomic experiences. Allow it to cast its spell on you, as it did on me, and create your own unique experience in this lovely corner of France.

Why Visit the Dordogne?

Dordogne, a location in the heart of France, entices visitors with its compelling attraction. If you're looking for a new place to visit, here are some strong reasons why Dordogne should be at the top of your list:

The Dordogne is a picturesque landscape right out of a fairy tale. Its natural splendor is nothing short of spectacular, from rolling vineyards and sunflower fields to twisting rivers and verdant woodlands. Every turn exposes a magnificent landscape, luring you into the tranquility and charm of the French countryside.

Rich History: Prepare to travel back in time as you discover Dordogne's historical riches. The area is peppered with medieval villages, each with its own distinct personality. Explore cobblestone alleys, appreciate historic architecture, and let your imagination run wild as you learn about knights, nobles, and ages gone by.

Majestic Châteaux: The Dordogne region is home to a number of beautiful castles that will take you to a realm of grandeur and wealth. Admire the architectural beauty of Château de Castelnaud, feel in awe of Château de Beynac's formidable walls, and lose yourself in the magnificent grounds of Château de Hautefort. These magnificent structures provide witness to the region's rich history.

Prehistoric Wonders: Visit the prehistoric sites of Dordogne to delve into the depths of human history. The UNESCO World Heritage Site of the Vézère Valley is a treasure trove of prehistoric cave paintings and relics. Explore the complex carvings of Font-de-Gaume and the prehistoric mammoth images of Rouffignac, as well as the awe-inspiring artistry of Lascaux. These prehistoric marvels offer an insight into the distant past.

Gastronomic Delights: Get ready for a culinary adventure in the Dordogne. The region is well-known for its culinary heritage, and it offers a wonderful assortment of flavors. Enjoy the earthy richness of truffles, the buttery goodness of foie gras, and the complexity of wines from the vineyards of Bergerac and Bordeaux. Dordogne is a foodie's heaven, with everything from rustic farm-to-table cuisine to Michelin-starred eateries.

Outdoor Adventures: The natural wonders of the Dordogne entice adventurers. Canoe down the Dordogne River, trek the Périgord Noir's picturesque paths, or soar to the skies in a hot air balloon for a bird's-eye view of the breathtaking scenery. Dordogne has plenty of opportunities to connect with nature, whether you prefer leisurely explorations or adrenaline-fueled adventures.

Warm Hospitality: Enjoy the warmth and friendliness of the Dordogne residents. Explore lively marketplaces where passionate traders display their regional produce and crafts. Engage in discussions with locals who are keen to share their passion for their region and its traditions. The people of Dordogne will bring an extra dimension of warmth and genuineness to your journey.

The Dordogne is a destination that will leave you speechless. This location has it all, whether you're looking for natural beauty, a glimpse into history, culinary delights, or outdoor adventures. Allow the Dordogne to enchant you and create treasured memories that will last a lifetime.

History and Culture Overview

Dordogne, located in southwestern France, is a region rich in history and culture. Dordogne's past has molded its identity and offers a wonderful tapestry of legacy for visitors to discover, from prehistoric civilizations through medieval periods and beyond.

Prehistoric Roots: The Dordogne's origins can be traced back to prehistoric times. The region is known for having an unusually high number of prehistoric sites, particularly in the Vézère Valley. Cave paintings, such as those found at Lascaux, Font-de-Gaume, and Rouffignac, provide us with an insight into our ancestors' lives and showcase their incredible artistic abilities. Dordogne is a monument to the area's lengthy human habitation, dating back tens of thousands of years.

Medieval Marvels: The medieval period in Dordogne left an everlasting stamp on the region. Its villages and towns are dotted with architectural marvels, ancient strongholds, and picturesque alleyways that have preserved their beauty over time. Sarlat-la-Canéda's well-preserved medieval core is a living witness to the region's rich history. Beynac-et-Cazenac, Domme, and Rocamadour are three other renowned medieval settlements, each with its own distinct history and allure.

Castles and Châteaux: The Dordogne region is home to a plethora of castles and châteaux that convey a sense of grandeur and intrigue. These architectural wonders, situated on cliffs or hidden among lush surroundings, transport tourists to a time of knights, feudal lords, and rich courtly life. The most well-known are Château de Castelnaud, Château de Beynac, and Château de Hautefort, which each offer a look into the region's medieval past.

Gastronomy and Culinary Heritage: The Dordogne is a foodie's paradise, known for its gourmet delights and culinary traditions. The region is famous for its truffles, sometimes known as "black gold," and foie gras, a delicacy made from fattened duck or goose liver. Fresh fruit, local cheeses, and handmade products abound in food markets, reflecting the region's rich agricultural background. Combine these gastronomic delights with Bergerac and Bordeaux wines for a sensory experience unlike any other.

Local Traditions and Festivals: The cultural heritage of Dordogne is alive and well in its local traditions and festivals. The region comes alive with lively celebrations, processions, and events that highlight its history, heritage, and artistic manifestations throughout the year. The medieval festivals of Sarlat and Domme, as well as religious pilgrimages to Rocamadour, offer a look into the region's cultural tapestry.

Warm Hospitality: The Dordogne is noted for the great friendliness of its people, in addition to its historical and cultural attractions. Visitors are welcomed with real warmth by the people, who share their tales, traditions, and passion for their land. Engaging with people, whether at markets, picturesque towns, or traditional festivals, allows visitors to build a stronger bond with the region and its dynamic culture.

Dordogne is rich in history, culture, and traditions. Dordogne offers an enriching experience that blends the past with the present, inviting visitors to embark on a captivating journey through time.

CHAPTER 1:
PLANNING YOUR TRIP TO DORDOGNE

Planning a trip to the lovely Dordogne area is a fascinating activity with limitless possibilities. The Dordogne, located in southwestern France, is a mesmerizing blend of natural beauty, ancient history, excellent food, and kind friendliness. This chapter will serve as your thorough guide to help you organize the perfect vacation to the Dordogne, whether you're a history buff, a nature lover, a gourmet aficionado, or simply looking for a memorable break.

In this chapter, we'll go through the essentials of trip planning, making sure that every detail is taken into account. We'll help you handle the logistics with ease, from selecting the best time to come and understanding weather trends to providing helpful information on transit alternatives and lodging recommendations. Our goal is to make your trip to the Dordogne as easy as possible, allowing you to focus on the wonders that await you.

Aside from the logistics, we'll go deep into the Dordogne, studying its many offerings through thematic chapters. You'll come across medieval villages that have been frozen in time, with cobblestone alleys whispering tales of bygone civilizations. The architectural magnificence of majestic châteaux will mesmerize you, transporting you through centuries of history. Prehistoric wonders will reveal the mysteries of cave art and transport you back in antiquity.

Outdoor adventures will call, encouraging you to canoe down tranquil rivers, hike through stunning scenery, and fly over valleys in hot air balloons. You'll sample the region's cuisine, including truffles, foie gras, and world-class wines that have given the Dordogne its gastronomic reputation.

We'll also immerse ourselves in local culture, from bustling markets bursting with smells and colors to traditional festivals honoring the region's past and craftsmanship. You'll be equipped to explore the Dordogne with confidence and respect thanks to practical knowledge and recommendations on etiquette, language, health, safety, and more.

Whether you're visiting for the first time or returning to discover new gems, this chapter will serve as your guide in planning an amazing trip to the Dordogne. Pack your luggage, open your heart to the wonders that await, and let the adventure begin as we embark on the journey of planning your dream trip to the enthralling Dordogne.

When to Visit Dordogne

The Dordogne region has a temperate climate, making it a popular vacation destination all year. However, the timing of your visit might have a significant impact on your overall experience. Each season has its own distinct appeal, and understanding weather trends and tourism seasons will assist you in planning your vacation properly.

The Dordogne is very beautiful in the spring (March to May). As flowers blossom, the landscapes come alive with brilliant colors, and the weather is nice. It's a great time for outdoor activities like hiking and exploring the gorgeous villages without the throngs of high season.

Because of the pleasant and sunny weather, summer (June to August) is the busiest tourist season in the Dordogne. The region is alive and well, with several cultural events, festivals, and marketplaces taking place. It's the ideal season to take leisurely boat trips on the Dordogne River, dine al fresco, and explore the many historical buildings and attractions. However, expect greater crowds and higher pricing throughout this period.

Autumn (September to November) in the Dordogne is a compelling season, with pleasant temperatures and gorgeous fall foliage. As the grapes ripen, the vineyards are a sight to behold, and it's an ideal time to indulge in local gastronomy, including harvest season delights. As the tourist crowds recede, the atmosphere becomes more serene and intimate.

The Dordogne is quieter in the winter (December to February). Despite the colder weather, the location keeps its attraction. It's the season for curling up by the fireplace in quaint lodgings, discovering fascinating ancient villages, and tasting hearty local cuisine. During this season, some attractions and restaurants may have limited working hours, so it's best to call ahead.

The best time to visit the Dordogne ultimately depends on your choices and interests. Consider the activities you want to do, your tolerance for crowds, and the weather you want. Whatever the season, the beauty and cultural richness of the Dordogne await, ensuring a wonderful visit.

How to Get to Dordogne

The Dordogne region is well-connected to many modes of transportation, making it easy to reach this wonderful destination. Whether you want to fly, take the train, or drive, there are several options for getting to the heart of the Dordogne.

By Air: Bergerac Dordogne Périgord Airport (EGC) is the closest international airport to the Dordogne. It has regular flights from various European towns, making it a popular travel destination. To get to your final location in the Dordogne, you can rent a car or take a cab from the airport.

Flying into Bordeaux-Mérignac Airport (BOD), which is well-connected to major cities globally, is another alternative. You can rent a car in Bordeaux and drive to the Dordogne (about a 2-hour drive) or take a train to one of the Dordogne's main train stations.

By Train: The Dordogne is easily reached by train from major French cities. Sarlat-la-Canéda, Bergerac, and Périgueux are the region's principal train stations. TGV trains run from Paris to Bordeaux, where you can change to a regional train to reach the Dordogne. The train journey provides travelers with stunning vistas of the French countryside and is a pleasant alternative.

By Car: Renting a car is a fantastic option to explore the Dordogne at your own leisure if you prefer the flexibility of driving. The region is well-served by motorways such as the A20 and A89, which connect to major French cities. Driving allows you to easily explore the Dordogne's lovely villages, châteaux, and natural features.

When you arrive in the Dordogne, having a car will help you explore the region. It allows you to go off the beaten path and uncover hidden jewels that would be difficult to reach by public transportation.

It's worth noting that public transportation in the Dordogne, such as buses, is scarce, particularly in rural areas. As a result, having a car increases your convenience and accessibility during your stay.

Getting Around in Dordogne

Exploring the scenic Dordogne region is a lovely experience, and there are a variety of transportation options available to assist you in navigating the area and making the most of your vacation.

Car Rental: Renting a car is a popular option for Dordogne visitors because it allows you to explore at your own speed. There are various automobile rental firms in the region, with locations at airports, train stations, and major towns. Having a car allows you to easily reach the Dordogne's picturesque villages, historical attractions, and natural wonders. Make sure you are familiar with the local driving norms and restrictions, and consider purchasing a GPS or using a navigation app to assist you in navigating the twisting country roads.

Public Transportation: While public transit is not as prevalent in the Dordogne as it is in larger towns, there are still choices for getting around. Buses run inside the major towns and connect some of the smaller villages, making it easy to commute between locations. Because bus schedules may be limited, it is best to check the timetables ahead of time.

Train: Another way to explore the Dordogne is by train. Regional trains connect the region's major towns and provide a convenient and scenic mode of transportation. Sarlat-la-Canéda, Bergerac, and Périgueux train stations are well connected to other cities in France.

Cycling and walking: The gorgeous landscapes and charming villages of the Dordogne make it an ideal destination for cycling and strolling. There are various biking and hiking routes that allow you to immerse yourself in the area's natural splendor. Many communities rent bikes, and guided riding trips are available if you prefer a more organized experience. Walking is a great way to explore the medieval villages' tiny alleyways and absorb the ambiance. Some communities even provide guided walking excursions that provide insights into the region's history and culture.

Guided Tours: A guided tour is a wonderful option, whether you prefer a hassle-free experience or want to learn more about the local culture and history. There are numerous tour operators in the Dordogne that offer guided tours ranging from day trips to multi-day excursions. These trips often include transportation, skilled guides, and visits to significant landmarks, resulting in an all-encompassing and enriching experience.

Getting around in the Dordogne, regardless of the means of transportation, allows you to discover the region's hidden gems, immerse yourself in its rich history and culture, and relish the stunning views at your own speed. Explore the enchantment of this region's winding roads, gorgeous villages, and compelling sites.

Where to Stay in Dordogne

The Dordogne region has a wide variety of lovely neighborhoods and towns where you can find appropriate accommodations to meet your needs. Each town has its own distinct personality and attractions, allowing you to pick the ideal base for your stay in this lovely region. Here are some of the best places to live:

Sarlat-la-Canéda: Known as the "Jewel of the Dordogne," Sarlat-la-Canéda is a magnificently maintained medieval village. Its charming ambience is created by its small cobblestone streets, half-timbered buildings, and bustling marketplaces. With its rich tradition and excellent eateries, this neighborhood is ideal for history buffs and foodies. Stay in Sarlat-la-Canéda to experience the medieval atmosphere and to visit neighboring attractions such as beautiful castles and prehistoric caverns.

Bergerac: A dynamic town noted for its wine production, Bergerac is located on the banks of the Dordogne River. This neighborhood is ideal for wine lovers because it provides opportunities to visit vineyards and partake in wine tastings. Bergerac also has a lovely old town with winding streets, tiny shops, and traditional eateries. Staying in Bergerac allows you to enjoy the region's distinctive cuisine as well as the riverfront landscape.

Beynac-et-Cazenac: Perched on a hilltop overlooking the Dordogne River, Beynac-et-Cazenac is a postcard-perfect village with a fairytale-like backdrop. This neighborhood is ideal for individuals seeking peace and breathtaking vistas. Explore the majestic Château de Beynac, take a stroll along the riverfront, and enjoy the tranquil atmosphere. Beynac-et-Cazenac accommodations frequently have spectacular views of the river and surrounding countryside.

Les Eyzies-de-Tayac-Sireuil: Known as the "Capital of Prehistory," this neighborhood in the Vézère Valley is a haven for archaeology buffs, with an abundance of prehistoric sites and museums. Learn about early human civilization by exploring the amazing caverns and rock shelters, including the famed Lascaux caves. Les Eyzies-de-Tayac-Sireuil has a variety of lodging options, ranging from small guesthouses to fancy hotels.

Périgueux: As the Dordogne's capital city, Périgueux mixes history, culture, and modern conveniences. The area is known for its well-preserved ancient town, which includes a stunning church, tiny alleyways, and charming squares. With its bustling markets, lively restaurants, and cultural events, Périgueux has a dynamic vibe. Stay in Périgueux for easy access to the region's attractions as well as a vibrant metropolitan experience.

These are just a few of the many Dordogne neighborhoods to consider while arranging your visit. Whether you prefer the medieval charm of Sarlat-la-Canéda, the wine tradition of Bergerac, or the calm serenity of Beynac-et-Cazenac, each neighborhood has its own distinct personality and a variety of lodgings to suit a variety of budgets and interests.

Choosing the Right Accommodation in Dordogne

When it comes to choosing the ideal Dordogne accommodation, there are lots of options to fit every traveler's needs and interests. Whether you're looking for elegance, charm, or a low-cost stay, here are some examples of the various sorts of accommodations available:

Charming Bed and Breakfasts: If you want to stay somewhere intimate and personalized, consider staying at a charming bed and breakfast. These hotels are frequently family-run and provide comfortable rooms, delectable breakfasts, and a welcoming ambiance. You'll be able to communicate with the welcoming hosts and obtain insider information on the best local activities and dining areas.

Historic Hotels: Staying in a historic hotel allows you to immerse yourself in the region's rich history. Dordogne has a number of magnificently renovated châteaux, manor homes, and medieval inns that have been converted into one-of-a-kind accommodations. These institutions provide a blend of modern comfort and old-world charm, allowing you to immerse yourself in the atmosphere of ages gone by.

Country Cottages: For a self-catering option and a home-away-from-home feel, consider renting a country cottage. These cottages, which are scattered around the countryside, offer privacy, space, and the opportunity to immerse yourself in the natural splendor of the Dordogne. They frequently include kitchen facilities, allowing you to create your own meals while enjoying the local produce.

Luxury Resorts: If you're looking for a relaxing and indulgent vacation, the Dordogne features luxury resorts with first-rate amenities and services. Spa facilities, excellent dining restaurants, and attractive settings surrounded by lush scenery are common features of these resorts. Enjoy a peaceful hideaway with all modern conveniences and exceptional service.

Budget-Friendly Accommodations: Travelers on a tight budget can also find economical accommodations in the Dordogne. There are budget hotels, hostels, and guesthouses that offer decent accommodations and basic facilities at a lower cost. These choices allow you to save money on lodging and spend it on discovering the region's attractions and enjoying its culinary delights.

Consider variables such as location, amenities, and your particular tastes while selecting the ideal lodging. Do you want a central location near attractions or a hidden country retreat? Are you looking for certain amenities, such as a swimming pool or an on-site restaurant? By taking these factors into account, you may locate the ideal lodging that enriches your Dordogne experience and gives you a comfortable and enjoyable stay.

Must-Visit Restaurants and Foods to Try

The Dordogne region is well-known for its superb gastronomic options, which include farm-to-table cuisine and regional delicacies. When visiting the Dordogne, make sure to eat the following scrumptious meals at the following must-visit restaurants:

Le Grand Bleu (Sarlat-la-Canéda): This Michelin-starred restaurant offers an outstanding dining experience in Sarlat-la-Canéda. Chef Pierre Corre demonstrates his culinary skills with inventive meals made with local resources. Each plate is a piece of art, from the superb seafood to the inventive sweets.

La Tour des Vents (Monbazillac): This restaurant, located in the lovely vineyards of Monbazillac, provides stunning vistas and superb gourmet cuisine. Enjoy a great lunch created with fresh, local products and matched by the region's famous sweet white wines.

Ferme Auberge de la Truffe (Sorges): Known as the "Black Truffle Capital," Sorges is a must-see for truffle fans. The Ferme Auberge de la Truffe serves classic truffle-based cuisine, allowing you to sample the wonderful flavors of this sought-after ingredient. For a true taste of the region, try the truffle omelet or truffle-infused pâté.

La Petite Tonnelle (Beynac-et-Cazenac): This restaurant, located in the picturesque village of Beynac-et-Cazenac, offers a delectable culinary experience. Sample regional delights like confit de canard or foie gras while admiring breathtaking views of the Dordogne River.

Les Jardins de Brantôme (Brantôme): This restaurant, located in the charming town of Brantôme, combines a stunning environment with excellent cuisine. Dishes are created using fresh, local ingredients, including trout from a nearby river. A wonderful eating experience is provided by the terrace overlooking the abbey.

Try the traditional dishes that highlight the flavors of the region when exploring the local cuisine. Try the rich foie gras, a delicacy prepared from duck or goose liver that is commonly served in terrines or with sweet fruit preserves. Shave earthy and aromatic black truffles over foods or integrate them into sauces and pâtés.

Don't miss out on the region's outstanding wines. Bergerac and Bordeaux wines are abundantly accessible and complement the local food wonderfully. There is a wine for every taste, from strong reds to delicate whites.

Whether you're looking for Michelin-starred meals or authentic regional flavors, the Dordogne has plenty to offer. Discover these must-see eateries and sample the region's culinary delights for a unique dining experience.

Must-Try Tour Activities in Dordogne

There are various tour activities that you should attempt when seeing the gorgeous Dordogne region. These activities are one-of-a-kind experiences that allow you to immerse yourself in the area's natural beauty, rich history, and cultural heritage. Here are some must-do Dordogne tour activities:

Canoeing on the Dordogne River: Take a picturesque canoe trip down the Dordogne River. Paddle through stunning scenery, past old castles, beautiful villages, and lush flora. It's a great chance to admire the natural beauty of the area while also discovering hidden jewels along the riverbanks.

Exploring Prehistoric Caves: The Dordogne region is home to a wonderful collection of prehistoric caves that display stunning cave art and signs of early human civilizations. Visit the famed Lascaux caves or other locations such as Font-de-Gaume and Rouffignac to see the stunning cave paintings and learn about our ancestors.

Hot Air Balloon Ride: For a truly beautiful experience, soar over the lovely landscapes of the Dordogne in a hot air balloon. From a unique vantage point, admire the magnificent castles, rolling hills, and flowing rivers. It's an unforgettable way to experience the beauty of the region and make lifelong memories.

Wine Tasting in Bergerac and Bordeaux: The Dordogne region is well-known for its outstanding wine districts, particularly Bergerac and Bordeaux. Take a wine tasting tour and sample the flavors of the region's wines. Visit vineyards, learn about the winemaking process, and sample red, white, and sweet wines with expert supervision.

Visiting Châteaux and Medieval Villages: Visit the majestic châteaux and medieval villages strewn throughout Dordogne to learn about the region's rich history and architectural treasures. From the majestic Château de Castelnaud to the charming village of Sarlat-la-Canéda, each location provides a peek into the region's history and allows you to travel back in time.

Gastronomic Tours: The Dordogne region is renowned for its exquisite cuisine and regional specialties. Take a gastronomy tour to enjoy the best of the region's products, including truffles, foie gras, and local cheeses. Visit lively markets, take cooking classes, and savor the flavors of the Dordogne.

These must-try tour activities in Dordogne provide a wide selection of experiences to suit a variety of interests and tastes. Dordogne has something for everyone, whether you're looking for adventure, cultural immersion, or culinary delights. In this intriguing region, embrace these activities and make great memories.

What to Pack for Your Trip to Dordogne

To ensure a comfortable and enjoyable trip to the Dordogne, it is important to pack accordingly. The following items should be on your packing list:

Clothing: Dordogne has a warm climate, but temperatures can vary throughout the year. Pack lightweight, breathable apparel, such as shorts, t-shirts, and skirts, for the summer months. Layers, such as light sweaters or jackets, are recommended for spring and autumn. If you're going in the winter, bring warm clothing such as coats, sweaters, and scarves.

Comfortable Shoes: The Dordogne is best explored on foot, so bring comfortable walking shoes or sneakers. Because you'll be walking through picturesque villages, exploring historical sites, and trekking scenic trails, you'll need dependable and supportive footwear.

Outdoor Gear: Pack suitable outdoor gear if you intend to engage in outdoor activities like canoeing or hiking. To protect yourself from the sun and bugs, bring a hat, sunglasses, sunscreen, and insect repellent. If you wish to take a relaxing plunge in the river or visit a local swimming hole, don't forget to pack a swimsuit.

Adapters and chargers: The Dordogne region uses the usual European two-pin plug, so bring adapters for your electronic equipment. Don't forget to pack chargers for your phone, camera, and other gadgets that will be used to capture and document your vacation.

Travel Documents: Keep all of your important travel documents organized and safe. This contains your passport, ID, travel insurance details, and any required visas. As a backup, it's a good idea to save digital copies of these papers on your phone or in cloud storage.

Backpack or Day Bag: A compact backpack or day bag will come in handy for transporting your things for day trips and excursions. It should be light and easy to carry, letting you keep your hands free while enjoying the sites.

Medications and First Aid Kit: If you require prescription medications, make sure you carry enough for the duration of your trip. Pack a modest first-aid kit with basic materials like bandages, painkillers, and any personal prescriptions or treatments you might need.

Remember to pack for the season and the activities you intend to participate in. It's also a good idea to check the local weather forecast before your journey in case you need any special apparel or accessories. You'll be well-prepared to make the most of your stay in Dordogne and have a wonderful journey if you pack wisely.

Entry and Visa Requirements

If you are considering a trip to Dordogne, it is critical that you understand the French entry and visa requirements, as Dordogne is located on French territory. Here are some crucial details to remember:

Passport Validity: Make sure your passport is valid for at least six months beyond your intended departure date from France. It is usually a good idea to check your passport's expiration date ahead of time and renew it if necessary.

Visa Requirement: France is a member of the Schengen Area, which allows travelers from numerous countries to enter without a visa for short-term stays. Visas are not required for citizens of the European Union (EU), the European Economic Area (EEA), or Switzerland to enter France or the Dordogne. If you are a non-EU or EEA citizen, you may need to apply for a Schengen visa before your trip. The particular visa requirements are determined by your country as well as the purpose and length of your travel.

Schengen Visa: If you need a Schengen visa, you should apply for one well in advance of your planned travel. A valid passport, travel itinerary, evidence of accommodation, travel insurance, and financial means to support your stay are normally required throughout the visa application procedure.

Travel Insurance: While travel insurance is not required for admission into France, it is highly suggested that you have comprehensive travel insurance that covers medical emergencies, trip cancellations, lost luggage, and other unforeseen occurrences. Before you travel, it is important to review your insurance coverage and ensure that it suits your needs.

Customs and Immigration: Upon arrival in France, you will be subjected to customs and immigration checks. Prepare all necessary paperwork, including your passport, visa (if applicable), and any supporting documentation asked for by the immigration officer. Prepare to answer questions about the reason for your visit, the length of your stay, and your planned activities in Dordogne.

It is important to check the most recent visa and entry requirements before your travel, as restrictions are subject to change. The information presented here is intended to serve as a basic guideline, but it is always advisable to contact the official websites of the French embassy or consulate in your country for the most accurate and up-to-date information regarding Dordogne entry and visa requirements.

Currency and Language

The Euro (€) is the official currency of France, including Dordogne. It's a good idea to keep extra cash in Euros on hand for little purchases, especially in rural areas where card payments aren't usually accepted. In Dordogne, ATMs are commonly available, allowing you to withdraw cash in local currencies. Major credit cards are frequently accepted in hotels, restaurants, and shops, but carrying cash for smaller establishments or markets is always a smart idea.

French is the official language of France and the major language spoken in the Dordogne. It can be useful to have a basic familiarity with common French phrases and greetings when visiting the Dordogne. Although English is spoken in many tourist places, hotels, and restaurants, guests who make an effort to communicate in French are always appreciated. Learning a few simple phrases like "hello" (bonjour), "thank you" (merci), and "excuse me" (excusez-moi) can go a long way toward improving your interactions with locals and demonstrating respect for local culture.

It should be noted that Dordogne is famed for its picturesque rural towns, and English proficiency among residents may be restricted in some remote locations. Dordogne's tourism business, on the other hand, is well-developed, and English-speaking workers may be found in tourist offices, hotels, and renowned tourist attractions.

In larger towns or cities, you can exchange currencies at banks or currency exchange agencies. Some post offices and tourist information centers may also provide money exchange services. It is wise to compare exchange rates and fees to get the most bang for your buck.

Carrying a small phrasebook or using language translation applications on your mobile device might also help you overcome any language problems you may face during your Dordogne visit.

You will improve your overall experience and interactions while touring the lovely Dordogne region if you are prepared with some local currency and have a basic knowledge of the French language and etiquette.

Suggested Budget

When planning a trip to the Dordogne, keep your budget in mind to ensure a comfortable and pleasurable experience. The total cost of your trip will be determined by a number of factors, including your travel preferences, accommodation choices, eating options, activities, and the duration of your stay. To help you estimate your budget, here is a general breakdown of expenses:

Accommodations: There are numerous options for accommodation available in Dordogne to meet a variety of budgets. There are luxurious hotels, lovely bed and breakfasts, self-catering cottages, and affordable guesthouses. Prices differ according to location and amenities. Mid-range lodgings will typically cost between €70 and €150 per night. Prices may be higher during peak tourist seasons, though.

Meals: Dordogne offers a wide range of dining alternatives, from Michelin-starred restaurants to local cafes and classic bistros. The cost of meals will vary depending on where you dine. A low-cost lunch at a casual restaurant or café may cost between €10 and €20 per person, whereas a three-course meal at a mid-range restaurant may cost between €25 and €40 per person. Exploring local markets and creating your own meals can also save money.

Transportation: Getting around the Dordogne will cost money. Consider the cost of flights to the nearest airport if you are arriving by air. Renting a car in the Dordogne is a popular option because it allows you to explore the region at your own pace. Rental car prices ;ary, however, a week's rental might cost between €200 and €400. Trains and buses, as well as other modes of public transit, are available and provide more economical options for traveling around.

Activities and Sightseeing: The Dordogne is famed for its historical sites, natural beauty, and outdoor activities. Admission to attractions such as castles, caves, and museums can cost between €5 and €15 per person. Outdoor activities like canoeing, hiking, and hot air balloon excursions may incur additional fees depending on the supplier and package you select. It is a good idea to investigate and prioritize the things that you are most interested in before allocating a budget.

Miscellaneous Expenses: Other expenses to consider include travel insurance, visa fees (if applicable), souvenirs, and any other personal charges. It is a good idea to save some money for unforeseen charges or spontaneous activities that may arise during your trip.

Keep in mind that the specified budget is only a guideline; actual expenses will vary depending on individual tastes and travel habits. It is essential that you conduct thorough price research, verify current exchange rates, and develop a detailed budget plan based on your individual trip needs and interests.

By properly planning and budgeting, you can make the most of your trip to the Dordogne and assure a wonderful time while staying within your financial means.

Money-Saving Tips

Dordogne exploration can be a pleasurable experience without breaking the bank. Here are some money-saving strategies to help you make the most of your trip while staying within your budget:

Travel during the shoulder season: Visit Dordogne during the spring (April to June) and fall (September to October) shoulder seasons. When compared to the high summer season, you can frequently get better discounts on accommodations and encounter fewer crowds during these periods.

Choose self-catering accommodations: Select lodgings that include a kitchen or kitchenette, such as self-catering flats or holiday rentals. This helps you save money on eating expenses by preparing some of your meals with local materials from markets or grocery stores.

Explore the local markets: Dordogne is known for its vibrant markets that sell fresh vegetables, regional delicacies, and artisanal goods. Instead of eating out every meal, visit these markets to pick up items for picnics or to enjoy economical local delights.

Pack a picnic: The Dordogne is blessed with stunning scenery that is ideal for outdoor picnics. Pack a picnic basket with local cheeses, bread, fruits, and other delicacies from the markets for a low-cost supper while admiring the scenery.

Take advantage of free or discounted attractions: The Dordogne region is home to a number of free or low-cost attractions, including picturesque villages, hiking trails, and natural sites. Plan trips to these locations to experience the region's charm without spending a bunch.

Use public transportation: If you are traveling alone or in small groups, public transit, including buses and trains, can be a more cost-effective alternative for traveling around Dordogne. Check the schedules and fares ahead of time to arrange your trip.

Look for discounted tickets or passes: Some attractions provide discounts for students, the elderly, and families.

Consider obtaining a regional pass or tourist card, which gives you cheap or free access to a variety of sites, transportation, or guided excursions.

Tap into local expertise: Engage with locals and ask for recommendations for economical dining alternatives, hidden gems, and local events taking place during your visit. They can offer valuable insights that can lead you to cost-effective yet authentic experiences.

Plan ahead of time: Research and book accommodations, transportation, and main attractions ahead of time to secure better rates and avoid last-minute price increases. Look for special discounts or discounted packages that will help you save money on your overall vacation costs.

You will have a fantastic trip to the Dordogne without breaking the bank if you follow these money-saving tips. Remember to prioritize your experiences, concentrate on the region's distinctive offerings, and embrace the local culture for an enriching and cost-effective trip.

Best Places to Book Your Trip

When it comes to booking your trip to Dordogne, there are various trustworthy platforms and tools to assist you in finding the best deals and planning your itinerary. Here are some of the best areas to start planning your trip:

Online Travel Agencies (OTAs): Popular platforms for booking flights, lodgings, and vehicle rentals include Expedia, Booking.com, and TripAdvisor. They provide a diverse selection of options, user ratings, and competitive pricing, allowing you to compare and select the best bargains.

Official Tourism Websites: Go to the official tourism websites for Dordogne or the towns and villages you intend to visit. These websites offer detailed information on attractions, lodging, events, and local recommendations. They may also provide booking services or access to reputable local providers.

Hotel and Accommodation Websites: Many Dordogne hotels and accommodations have their own websites where you may book your stay directly. This can occasionally provide additional perks such as exclusive bargains, loyalty awards, or unique bundles. Consider visiting the websites of certain hotels or chains that pique your interest.

Vacation Rental Platforms: Platforms such as Airbnb, Vrbo, and HomeAway provide a diverse choice of vacation rentals, including apartments, cottages, and villas. These alternatives to standard hotels can be interesting and often cost-effective, especially for families or large groups.

Specialty Tour Operators: If you prefer a more curated and guided experience, consider booking with a Dordogne or surrounding region specialty tour company. These companies provide pre-planned itineraries, experienced guides, and access to one-of-a-kind experiences and local insights.

Local Travel Agencies: Connecting with local Dordogne travel agencies or tour operators can provide personalized help and tailored itineraries depending on your preferences. They may assist in arranging transportation, lodging, and activities, as well as providing insider information for an authentic and hassle-free trip.

Package Deals and Bundles: Look for package deals that incorporate accommodation, flights, and occasionally additional features like tours or transportation. When compared to booking each component separately, these packages can often offer cost savings.

When booking your trip, remember to compare costs, read reviews, and take into account your personal travel preferences and requirements. Booking ahead of time is always a smart idea, especially during busy travel seasons. You can plan and book your Dordogne trip with confidence and easily if you use the right resources and platforms.

CHAPTER 2:
EXPLORING THE MEDIEVAL VILLAGES

As we embark on a mesmerizing tour through the historic villages of Dordogne, we will enter a world locked in time. This chapter will transport you to a bygone era, complete with cobblestone streets, historic architecture, and a rich history. These villages will immerse you in a realm of medieval splendor, from the perfectly preserved Sarlat-la-Canéda, which embodies the essence of medieval life, to the awe-inspiring Beynac-et-Cazenac, where history comes alive before your eyes, and the enchanting Domme, perched high above the Dordogne River.

You'll walk through meandering passageways flanked by centuries-old buildings in Sarlat-la-Canéda, discovering the town's medieval legacy at every corner. The charming squares, exquisite residences, and imposing Saint-Sacerdos Cathedral will take you back in time, allowing you to feel the atmosphere of a bustling medieval market town.

Prepare to be captivated by Beynac-et-Cazenac's spectacular location and towering castle. With its towering fortress overlooking the Dordogne River, this hamlet provides a glimpse into feudal times. Explore the winding alleyways, appreciate the lovely stone cottages, and envision the stories of chivalry and courtly life that once took place behind these historic walls.

Finally, we rise to the hilltop village of Domme, a bastide town with stunning views of the Dordogne River valley. Domme, perched high above the terrain, emanates regality and tranquility. Explore its defensive walls, pay a visit to the gorgeous Notre-Dame-de-l'Assomption church, and take in the breathtaking views that spread as far as the eye can see.

This chapter will dig into the history, architecture, and distinctive features of these medieval communities. Join us as we unearth the legends of Sarlat-la-Canéda, Beynac-et-Cazenac, and Domme, as well as the secrets of Dordogne's enthralling history.

Sarlat-la-Canéda: A Journey Through Time

Enter the enchanted land of Sarlat-la-Canéda, where time stops and the past comes to life. This medieval jewel in the heart of the Dordogne takes you on a trip through centuries of history, art, and culture. Sarlat-la-Canéda, with its magnificently preserved architecture and busy marketplaces, provides a truly immersive excursion into the medieval past.

You'll be transported back in time as you walk through the maze of narrow cobblestone streets. Sarlat-la-Canéda's architectural marvels are a tribute to its rich legacy. Admire the beautifully carved facades, stately stone mansions, and timber-framed structures that have withstood the test of time. Every step exposes a new architectural jewel, prompting you to marvel at the medieval period's craftsmanship and attention to detail.

Sarlat-la-Canéda's bustling market scene is one of its features. Step into the lively marketplace, where local traders proudly display their abundant food, aromatic truffles, and handcrafted goods. Engage in friendly chats with the passionate sellers, sample the regional cuisines, and soak up the lively ambiance that has been a part of Sarlat-la-Canéda's appeal for decades. The market is not only a shopping destination but also a meeting area for locals and visitors, producing a tapestry of sights, sounds, and fragrances.

Sarlat-la-Canéda is well-known for its strong cultural scene, in addition to its architectural marvels and bustling marketplaces. Throughout the year, the town hosts a number of festivals and events in which the medieval spirit is commemorated in great style. Sarlat-la-Canéda has a rich cultural calendar that highlights its customs, culinary, and artistic legacy, from the Fest'Oie, a festival dedicated to the region's famous geese, to the Truffle Festival, where the treasured black truffle takes center stage.

Sarlat-la-Canéda welcomes you to travel back in time and immerse yourself in a world of medieval magnificence. Lose yourself in its picturesque streets, experience the flavors of the market, and take part in the town's active cultural events.

Beynac-et-Cazenac: Where History Comes Alive

As you enter the enchanting village of Beynac-et-Cazenac, you will be taken to a realm of knights, medieval lords, and legendary tales. This medieval jewel, perched magnificently on a cliff above the Dordogne River, evokes mystery and grandeur. Beynac-et-Cazenac, with its well-preserved architecture and awe-inspiring castle, provides an immersive experience where history truly comes alive.

The majestic Château de Beynac is the crowning beauty of Beynac-et-Cazenac. The castle's towering presence, perched on a rocky cliff, is enough to steal your breath away. As you make your way up the winding route to the castle, you'll feel the weight of centuries of history bear down on you. Inside, you'll learn about medieval life, from the formidable defensive buildings to the exquisite living rooms that formerly housed the noble occupants. The panoramic views from the castle's walls are breathtakingly breathtaking, revealing the strategic significance of this mighty bastion.

Beynac-et-Cazenac, beyond the castle, entices with its lovely streets and medieval architecture. The stone cottages in the town, covered with beautiful flowers, provide a gorgeous environment that appears to be fixed in time. Get lost in the labyrinthine lanes, where each turn unveils a new architectural masterpiece or a look into the people's daily lives. You'll find tiny artisan stores, pleasant cafes, and the warm friendliness of the residents, who are eager to share the stories and traditions of their beloved hamlet while you explore.

Beynac-et-Cazenac is more than just a historical site; it also has a thriving cultural scene. The village hosts a variety of events and festivals throughout the year to commemorate its medieval heritage. Visitors can immerse themselves in the ambiance of the past through reenactments of historical conflicts and medieval fairs that feature traditional crafts and arts. The rich history and cultural events of the town combine to produce an experience that is both educational and captivating.

Domme: Perched High Above the Dordogne

The hilltop village of Domme, perched high above the Dordogne River, provides a really magnificent experience. Domme captivates visitors from the moment they arrive with its commanding views, fortified walls, and attractive streets. This bastide village is a testimony to medieval inventiveness and architectural magnificence, beckoning you to explore its treasures and soak up the enchanting atmosphere.

The first thing that draws your attention to Domme is its breathtaking views. The community boasts panoramic views that go as far as the eye can see from its vantage point. View the Dordogne River valley, with its rolling hills, luscious vineyards, and lovely scenery. The breathtaking grandeur of the environment, mixed with the tranquility of the village, creates an incomparable sensation of serenity.

As you travel deeper into Domme, you'll come upon the village's fortified walls, a tribute to the village's strategic importance throughout history. Stroll along the walls, following the path that was previously defended by knights and soldiers. The walls not only provide a peek into the village's defensive heritage, but they also afford some of the most spectacular views of the surrounding countryside. From these heights, you'll acquire a fresh appreciation for medieval defenses' resourcefulness.

You'll find a lovely maze of alleyways within the village, replete with stone buildings covered with bright flowers. Domme's architecture reflects the city's long history, with structures reaching back centuries. Explore the Place de la Halle, the principal square where residents have congregated for years. Admire the delicate features that adorn the majestic Notre-Dame-de-l'Assomption church, with its elegant Gothic architecture.

Domme is not simply a historical site but also a bustling center for art and culture. There are various galleries and workshops throughout the hamlet where local artists can demonstrate their ability and ingenuity. Domme has a wide and dynamic art culture, ranging from classic paintings and sculptures to contemporary works. Take the time to explore these unique settings, and you'll be intrigued by the local craftsmen's talent and passion.

Time appears to stand still in Domme as you immerse yourself in a world of medieval grandeur and natural beauty. The village invites you to enter a sphere of peace and enchantment, from its commanding views to its guarded walls and lovely streets. If you embrace the Domme spirit, you will be rewarded with memories that will last a lifetime.

CHAPTER 3:
MAJESTIC CHÂTEAUX

As we delve into the Dordogne's beautiful châteaux, prepare to be lost in a world of grandeur and majesty. These architectural marvels will transport you to a time of feudal lords, extravagant dinners, and love tales, each with its own unique story and attraction. This chapter offers a glimpse into the wealthy world of Dordogne's châteaux, from the legendary Château de Castelnaud, a castle steeped in history, to the intriguing Château de Beynac, a medieval masterpiece located on a cliff, and the beautiful Château de Hautefort, where opulence reigns supreme.

Our adventure begins at the magnificent Château de Castelnaud, a castle that has witnessed centuries of legends and warfare. Explore its enormous walls, go through the medieval apartments, and learn about its history. Château de Castelnaud offers an immersive experience that will take you to a time of knights and sieges, from the historic armory that displays an astonishing collection of weaponry to the interactive exhibits that bring the castle's history to life.

We'll also delve into the magnificent Château de Beynac, a medieval masterpiece perched on a rock overlooking the Dordogne River. The castle's commanding position and stunning silhouette make it a sight to behold. Step inside its defended walls, explore the labyrinthine chambers, and envision the grandeur of the great family who once resided here. Château de Beynac offers a voyage into the heart of medieval life, from the panoramic views of the river valley to the well-preserved architectural elements.

Finally, we come across the magnificent Château de Hautefort, which is the epitome of beauty and refinement. This fairytale-like palace is set among carefully groomed grounds and is a sight to behold. Step inside and be enchanted by the opulent interiors, which are embellished with elaborate tapestries, ornate furnishings, and stunning artwork.

This chapter will dig into the enthralling histories, architectural marvels, and enthralling atmospheres of these magnificent châteaux. Discover the allure of Dordogne's big estates as we uncover the history behind Château de Castelnaud, Château de Beynac, and Château de Hautefort.

Château de Castelnaud: A Legendary Fortress

Explore the spectacular Château de Castelnaud to enter a world of medieval magnificence. This citadel, perched majestically on a hilltop overlooking the Dordogne River, is steeped in history and folklore. Château de Castelnaud, with its majestic architecture and rich collection of weaponry, provides an enthralling view into Dordogne's stormy past.

As you approach the castle, you'll be struck by its foreboding walls and towers, which attest to its defensive capabilities. Step beyond the gates, and you'll find yourself in a world trapped in time, with echoes of the past whispering through the hallways. Inside, you'll find an outstanding armory housing one of Europe's most significant collections of medieval weapons. The walls are adorned with swords, crossbows, and suits of armor, providing a real link to the fights and conflicts that formed the region's history.

Aside from its military significance, Château de Castelnaud provides tourists with a thorough and immersive experience. The castle's history is brought to life with interactive exhibitions and multimedia displays, allowing you to follow in the footsteps of knights and nobles who once roamed these halls. Discover medieval battle methods, watch a trebuchet demonstration, and delve into the remarkable tales of valor and chivalry that define the castle's past.

Château de Castelnaud is a tribute to the surviving spirit of the medieval age, from its strategic site above the Dordogne River to its amazing collection of weapons and interesting exhibits. Whether you're a history buff, a devotee of medieval folklore, or simply fascinated by architectural marvels of the past, a visit to this castle of legends will leave you in awe and spark your creativity.

The Château de Beynac: A Medieval Wonder

Prepare to be enchanted by the magnificent Château de Beynac, a medieval wonder that transports you to the period of knights and feudal lords. This spectacular castle, perched high on a cliff above the gorgeous Dordogne River, is a testimony to the architectural brilliance of the Middle Ages. Château de Beynac, with its imposing silhouette and rich historical significance, is a must-see for anybody looking to immerse themselves in the medieval beauty of the Dordogne.

The sight of Château de Beynac's fortified walls and towers will steal your breath away as you approach. Climb the winding road up to the castle's entryway for panoramic views of the surrounding landscape. Explore the labyrinthine tunnels, wander around the ramparts, and marvel at the architectural elements that have weathered the test of time once inside. Every nook of Château de Beynac offers a narrative of the past, from the medieval dwelling quarters to the defensive buildings that previously protected the castle.

The interior of the castle takes you to a bygone era of feudal beauty. Admire the magnificent tapestries that adorn the walls, the opulent furniture that exudes regal splendor, and the meticulously preserved objects that provide glimpses into daily life hundreds of years ago. Château de Beynac offers an immersive experience that allows you to imagine the grandeur and sophistication of medieval aristocracy, from the vast hall that hosted opulent dinners to the intricate decorations of the church.

Château de Beynac is not only a magnificent marvel but also a historical treasure trove. It was previously the home of the great Beynac family and played an important part in the Hundred Years' War. The castle served as a symbol of authority and was a monument to the political environment of the period, thanks to its strategic location and imposing presence.

Château de Beynac represents medieval architectural splendor and historical intrigue. Its commanding position, stunning architecture, and interesting history make it a must-see for history buffs and anyone looking to be transported to a world of knights and chivalry.

Château de Hautefort: Where Elegance Reigns

The beautiful Château de Hautefort reigns supreme as a symbol of elegance and refinement among the rolling hills of the Dordogne area. This beautiful castle, with its exquisite architecture, meticulously groomed gardens, and opulent interiors, offers a look into a world of royal magnificence and ageless beauty. Prepare to be swept away by Château de Hautefort's charm, where every detail emanates a feeling of grandeur.

Approaching Château de Hautefort is akin to entering a fairytale. The magnificent silhouette of the castle rises majestically above the surrounding countryside, producing an enthralling spectacle that leaves tourists speechless. You'll be greeted by a symphony of vivid hues and fragrant blooms as you stroll through the perfectly managed gardens. The grounds of Château de Hautefort are a tribute to the brilliance of landscape architecture, from the mathematically structured French gardens to the wild beauty of the English-style park.

If you enter the castle, you will be transported to a realm of polished beauty. Exquisite tapestries, elaborate furnishings, and superb artwork fill the magnificent interiors, reflecting the taste and elegance of the noble families that once called this palace home. Admire the rich features of the grand halls and chambers, and envision the magnificent balls and sumptuous meals held within these walls. Château de Hautefort's magnificence is bound to create an impression.

Beyond its architectural magnificence, Château de Hautefort provides insight into the region's cultural and historical legacy. Discover the castle's rich history through intriguing exhibitions and displays that showcase stories and objects from its past. Château de Hautefort weaves a tapestry of history that is as intriguing as it is engaging, from its strategic importance during the Hundred Years' War to its transition into a place of healing with the construction of a renowned medical hospital.

Château de Hautefort is a tribute to the past's continuing elegance and exquisite taste. Its beautiful architecture, lush grounds, and engaging interiors create a sophisticated and enchanting ambiance.

CHAPTER 4:
PREHISTORIC WONDERS

Take a trip back in time as we explore the fascinating chapter on Dordogne's prehistoric wonders. This chapter transports you back thousands of years to a time when ancient civilizations thrived and left a rich heritage of art and culture behind.

Our journey begins in the Vézère Valley, an archaeological treasure trove that offers a glimpse into the lives of our forefathers. This gorgeous valley is lined with numerous archaeological structures, including caves and rock shelters, that bear evidence of early human civilizations' rich cultural history.

We'll also visit the world-renowned caves of Lascaux and Font-de-Gaume, where the mysteries of cave art are revealed before our eyes. Enter these subterranean kingdoms and behold the awe-inspiring beauty of vibrantly colored paintings and intriguing symbols. Lascaux, also known as the "Sistine Chapel of Prehistoric Art," is a breathtaking display of ancient artistic ability, whereas

Font-de-Gaume reveals its secrets in an intimate and authentic setting.

Our tour of the prehistoric treasures of Dordogne concludes with a visit to the spectacular Rouffignac Cave, an underground sanctuary covered with mammoth engravings. This incredible site transports us to a time when these great creatures walked the planet, giving us a glimpse into the ancient fascination with these awe-inspiring species. Explore the cave's meandering chambers, marvel at the sheer quantity of carvings, and consider the relevance of these depictions in prehistoric culture.

In this chapter, we shall embark on an enthralling study of the prehistoric treasures of the Dordogne. Prepare to be surprised by our prehistoric ancestors' creativity, ingenuity, and cultural depth, and to experience firsthand the enduring legacy they left behind.

The Vézère Valley: A Gateway to the Past

Travel through the amazing Vézère Valley, a true gateway to the past, to enter a world of ancient treasures. This scenic Dordogne valley is famous for its archaeological treasures, which provide a fascinating view into the lives and cultures of our prehistoric predecessors. The Vézère Valley offers a compelling voyage through time, with breathtaking cave art and astonishing traces of early communities.

As you travel through the Vézère Valley, you will come across various archaeological sites that have helped form our understanding of prehistoric life. The valley has a large number of caves and rock shelters, many of which are decorated with elaborate paintings, engravings, and sculptures. These artistic creations provide important insights into the ancient inhabitants' beliefs, rituals, and daily lives who formerly called this region home. Discover the progression of artistic techniques, marvel at the artwork's fine intricacies, and ponder the importance of these ancient masterpieces.

Aside from its aesthetic riches, the Vézère Valley is home to a plethora of archaeological sites that allow an in-depth look into past cultures. Explore the ruins of old communities like Les Eyzies-de-Tayac, which serve as testaments to our forefathers' inventiveness and resourcefulness. Discover the evidence of their daily activities, from toolmaking to fire-making, and obtain a better appreciation of the difficulties they faced and the extraordinary achievements they made in a world vastly different from our own.

The Vézère Valley is a monument to our prehistoric past's continuing fascination. It encourages us to embark on an enthralling voyage through time to experience the craftsmanship, ingenuity, and cultural diversity of the ancient civilizations that once lived here. Whether you are interested in archaeology, history, or simply the mysteries of the past, the Vézère Valley offers a genuinely memorable experience that will improve your understanding of the wonderful fabric of human history.

Lascaux: Unravel the Mysteries of Cave Art

As you enter the legendary caves of Lascaux, you will enter a realm of astounding beauty and ancient intrigue. Lascaux, located in the heart of the Dordogne area, is a tribute to our prehistoric ancestors' great artistic abilities. These remarkable caves, found by chance in 1940, provide a hypnotic peek into the realm of cave art and vital insights into the rich cultural history of early human civilizations.

As you explore the depths of Lascaux, you'll be surrounded by a plethora of bright paintings that grace the cave walls. These ancient artworks stun visitors with their detailed intricacies, vibrant hues, and astounding realism. Animals such as horses, bison, deer, and a variety of other creatures come to life before your eyes, demonstrating our distant ancestors' remarkable artistic aptitude and great observation skills.

Unraveling Lascaux's riddles is an enthralling journey of discovery. Archaeologists and art historians have spent decades deciphering the meaning of these cave paintings and unraveling the stories they tell. Each brushstroke and symbol offers a tantalizing look into the beliefs, habits, and daily lives of the folks who created these awe-inspiring masterpieces, ranging from theories of ceremonial activities to hunting ceremonies.

A journey to Lascaux is an immersion into the very essence of human creativity, not just an examination of art. The ambiance of the cave, the flickering light, and the palpable connection to our ancient past all contribute to an atmosphere of awe and reverence. It is an opportunity to be in the presence of a legacy that spans thousands of years and to reflect on the tremendous relationship that humanity has with the artistic expression that has characterized our existence.

Lascaux is a tribute to art's enduring power and universal appeal. Visitors from all over the world are captivated and inspired by its elaborate artwork, hidden symbolism, and ethereal beauty.

Font-de-Gaume: A Glimpse into Ancient Life

Prepare to be taken back in time as you enter the incredible Font-de-Gaume cave, a location that provides an enthralling peek into the lives of our prehistoric forefathers. Font-de-Gaume, in France's Dordogne region, is famed for its well-preserved collection of prehistoric cave art, offering a rare opportunity to connect with the ancient cultures that previously thrived in the area.

Enter the depths of Font-de-Gaume and immerse yourself in a realm of artistic genius. The cave is covered with a wealth of amazing paintings of animals such as bison, mammoths, reindeer, and horses. The accuracy and skill demonstrated in these ancient artworks are breathtaking, offering a tribute to our prehistoric ancestors' creative talent and deep knowledge of the natural world.

Font-de-Gaume is distinguished by its authenticity and familiarity. Font-de-Gaume, unlike other well-known cave art sites, has not been copied or recreated. The paintings you see are real works of art that were made thousands of years ago. This unique and untouched experience allows you to interact with the past on a highly personal level, as if you were following in the footsteps of the painters who left their mark on the cave walls.

Aside from its artistic significance, Font-de-Gaume provides vital insights into our forefathers' daily lives and habits. The cave's distinctive features, including carvings, handprints, and abstract symbols, provide insights into prehistoric spiritual beliefs and practices. Each brushstroke and etching bears the weight of history, inviting you to decipher the stories and meanings hidden inside these ancient works of art.

A visit to Font-de-Gaume is a completely immersive experience, allowing you to observe the creativity, marvel at the preservation, and sense a tangible connection to our distant past. It is an opportunity to get a profound understanding of our prehistoric ancestors' rich cultural history and to respect the ongoing impact of their artistic talents.

Rouffignac: Exploring the Cave of the Hundred Mammoths

Prepare for an astonishing voyage as you explore the enthralling depths of Rouffignac Cave, a riveting location that reveals a remarkable chapter of prehistoric history. Rouffignac, in France's Dordogne area, is famous for its wealth of gigantic engravings, making it a genuine treasure trove for anyone wanting to uncover the mysteries of our ancient past.

Step inside the cold, darkly lit tunnels of Rouffignac Cave, and you'll be surrounded by an incredible exhibition of enormous engravings. Over a hundred images of these magnificent creatures adorn the cave walls, creating an immersive experience that transports you back in time to a time when these huge beasts roamed the Earth. The engravings' precision and detail are astonishing, capturing the essence of these long-extinct species and providing a vivid insight into their world.

While exploring the meandering corridors of Rouffignac Cave, you will come across not only mammoth engravings but also a rich array of other prehistoric artwork. The cave's walls bore testament to our ancient ancestors' remarkable artistic talents, from horses and bison to reindeer and rhinoceroses. Each engraving bears witness to their deep connection with nature and desire to leave a lasting legacy of their presence.

Rouffignac's significance extends beyond its cultural riches. The archaeological remnants discovered within the cave's chambers show that it acted as a shelter and refuge for prehistoric humans. Investigate the ruins of hearths, tools, and other relics that provide significant insights into our forefathers' daily lives and customs. Learn how people used the cave's resources and sought refuge beneath its depths, forming a unique link between humans and this natural sanctuary.

A visit to Rouffignac is an enthralling voyage through time, where you can see the incredible engravings, immerse yourself in the world of prehistoric mammoths, and obtain better knowledge of the complex relationship between humans and their environment.

CHAPTER 5:
OUTDOOR ADVENTURES

Immerse yourself in a world of amazing outdoor adventures as you embark on a thrilling exploration of the great outdoors in the Dordogne. This chapter will take you on a tour across the region's different landscapes and natural beauties, offering a variety of activities that will pique your interest and deliver an amazing experience.

Canoeing along the Dordogne River allows you to experience the quiet beauty of the river. Glide over its tranquil waters, surrounded by rich flora and stunning landscapes. Navigate across this quiet canal to discover hidden caves, lovely villages, and majestic châteaux that border the riverbanks.

The Périgord Noir region provides a wealth of hiking routes that run through its gorgeous landscapes for anyone looking for a land-based adventure. Lace up your hiking boots and explore this natural playground filled with old forests, rolling hills, and secret valleys. Immerse yourself in nature's splendor, breathe in fresh air, and discover hidden treasures along the road. Whether you're a seasoned hiker or a first-time adventurer, the Périgord Noir trails guarantee a voyage of natural beauty and spectacular landscapes.

Take to the skies on a hot-air balloon trip for a truly magical experience. Climb to the heights and watch the Dordogne Valley unfold beneath you like a patchwork quilt. Admire the undulating scenery, winding river, and charming settlements dotting the horizon. A hot air balloon journey provides a unique viewpoint and a sensation of awe-inspiring freedom, affording a bird's-eye view of the region's various splendors.

Prepare to experience the excitement of outdoor adventure in Dordogne by canoeing down the Dordogne River, hiking through the magnificent trails of Périgord Noir, and flying high above the valley in a hot air balloon. Each activity provides its own distinct blend of excitement, peace, and natural beauty, ensuring that outdoor enthusiasts and nature lovers alike will feel their hearts racing and their spirits soar.

Canoeing the Dordogne: A Serene River Escape

Set out on a peaceful voyage down the Dordogne River, taking in the calm and natural beauty that this wonderful waterway has to offer. Canoeing the Dordogne is more than simply a fun activity; it's an invitation to reconnect with nature, unwind, and embrace a sense of peace as you float over its soft currents. This tranquil river hideaway promises an amazing trip with its emerald- green rivers, verdant riverbanks, and scenic surroundings.

As you go off on your canoeing adventure, you'll be welcomed by a stunning landscape. Majestic limestone cliffs rise from the riverbanks, decorated with lush vegetation that creates a colorful tapestry. Admire the picturesque towns that border the shoreline, their exquisite stone cottages reflected in the calm seas. Immerse yourself in the calm rhythm of the river as you traverse its twists and turns, discovering hidden alcoves and secret caverns.

Canoeing the Dordogne provides not only a gorgeous escape but also an opportunity to learn about the region's rich history and culture. Drift past majestic medieval châteaux, quiet witnesses of a bygone era. Admire their magnificence and envision the stories of knights and noble families who once lived within their walls. Stop at riverbank cafes and eat the excellent native cuisine, tasting flavors developed over decades.

Whether you're a seasoned paddler or a first-time canoeist, the Dordogne River offers a tranquil and approachable experience for all. Whether you opt for a leisurely half-day trip or a multi-day adventure, the river provides a soothing flow that allows you to relax and take in the beauty of your surroundings. Canoeing the Dordogne is a gateway to peace, a chance to escape the hustle and bustle of daily life and find consolation in nature's embrace. So grab a paddle, immerse yourself in the tranquility of the Dordogne River, and allow its gentle currents to take you on an incredible journey of serenity and discovery.

Hiking the Périgord Noir: Trails of Natural Beauty

Set off on an enthralling journey through the picturesque landscapes of Périgord Noir, where hiking paths beckon with natural beauty and untamed wilderness. This Dordogne region is a haven for outdoor enthusiasts, with a vast network of paths winding through lush forests, rolling hills, and secret valleys. Lace up your hiking boots, take a deep breath of the crisp mountain air, and let the trails lead you through a world of breathtaking natural treasures.

Step into the well-marked paths of Périgord Noir, and you'll encounter a world of pristine beauty at every turn. You'll be surrounded by towering oak trees as you walk the pathways, their leaves fluttering in the pleasant breeze. As you walk through this magnificent woodland, sunlight streams through the canopy, leaving a mottled glow on the forest floor. Discover hidden waterfalls pouring down moss-covered rocks, stumble across quiet lakes reflecting the surrounding foliage, and meet the region's diverse flora and wildlife.

Périgord Noir hiking routes cater to all levels of expertise and fitness, guaranteeing that there is a path for everyone to enjoy. These routes allow you to immerse yourself in the natural splendor of the region at your own speed, from leisurely strolls down moderate slopes to strenuous ascents that reward you with panoramic landscapes.

You may come across delightful communities nestled in the landscapes along the journey, where you can relax, refuel, and absorb the local charm. Experience the region's gastronomic pleasures, fine wines, and warm hospitality of the inhabitants, adding a cultural dimension to your hiking journey.

Hiking the Périgord Noir is about reconnecting with nature, reviving your spirit, and embracing the therapeutic benefits of the great outdoors. The trails of Périgord Noir offer a portal to natural beauty that will leave you inspired, refreshed, and with memories to last a lifetime, whether you desire solitude and reflection or a shared experience with friends and loved ones.

Hot Air Balloon Rides: A Bird's-Eye View of the Valley

Delve into an unusual experience that will take you high above the Dordogne Valley, giving you a beautiful bird's-eye view of the region's magnificent surroundings. Hot air balloon rides provide a unique and exhilarating experience, allowing you to see the valley from a completely different perspective. Prepare to be enthralled as you softly soar into the sky, leaving behind the earth below and entering a universe of breathtaking landscapes.

The air is filled with excitement and expectation as the hot air balloon takes flight. Look out over the magnificent countryside, where rolling hills, lush vineyards, and meandering rivers create a picture-perfect canvas. From this vantage point, the Dordogne Valley reveals its natural beauties, exhibiting a mosaic of hues and textures that reach as far as the eye can see. Admire the splendor of the châteaux that dot the countryside, their turrets and towers boldly standing amidst the verdant surroundings.

Drift with the calm breeze, guided by the wind currents, and enjoy a serene and peaceful ride above the valley. Immerse yourself in the tranquility of the moment as you glide through the air, surrounded by nothing but the immense expanse of sky and the stunning landscapes below. As the balloon flies you over picturesque villages, meandering rivers, and sweeping forests, take in the splendor of the changing panorama. Each instant is a sensory overload, a visual symphony of colors and shapes that will stay with you forever.

A hot air balloon flight in the Dordogne Valley is more than simply a thrilling adventure; it's a chance to experience a sense of freedom and wonder. It's an opportunity to disengage from the world below and reconnect with the immensity of the sky and the magnificence of nature. It's a voyage that goes beyond the mundane, providing a unique perspective that will leave you in awe of the region's natural beauty and fill your heart with awe and inspiration.

So climb onboard the hot air balloon, brace yourself for an incredible trip, and see the Dordogne Valley unfold before you in all its glory.

CHAPTER 6:
GASTRONOMY OF THE DORDOGNE

Indulge your taste buds and embark on a culinary tour through the Dordogne's gastronomic wonders. This chapter honors the region's rich culinary legacy, with each taste telling a tale of tradition, passion, and the finest ingredients. The Dordogne welcomes you to appreciate its flavors and experience the creativity of its gastronomy, from the famed truffles to the exquisite foie gras and world-class wines.

Prepare to be enchanted by the appeal of truffles, known as the region's black gold. Explore the mysterious world of truffle hunting, where professional truffle hunters and their devoted dogs go out to find these prized treasures in the dirt. Discover the earthy and aromatic flavors of truffles as they add a touch of indulgence to the culinary creations of skilled chefs.

As we continue our culinary journey, we come across beautiful foie gras, a delicacy renowned for its creamy and buttery texture. Enjoy the velvety smoothness of this gastronomic delicacy as it melts on your tongue, leaving a symphony of tastes behind. Foie gras takes center stage in the Dordogne's culinary scene, from traditional preparations to contemporary interpretations, demonstrating the region's commitment to preserve age-old traditions while embracing culinary innovation.

Raise your glass and salute to perfection with the renowned Bergerac and Bordeaux wines to round out the dining experience. Explore the landscape's vineyards, where devoted winemakers methodically brew their wines with precision and competence. Allow the flavors to dance on your tongue as you experience the richness and character that each sip delivers, from the strong reds to the crisp whites.

Get ready for a gastronomic tour of the Dordogne, where truffles, foie gras, and wines take center stage. Indulge in the flavors that distinguish the region, learn about traditions passed down through generations, and discover the true essence of Dordogne gastronomy.

Truffles: The Black Gold of the Region

Immerse yourself in the enchantment of truffles, the black gold that has a unique place in the Dordogne's heart. Truffles have long been recognized as one of the world's most sought-after culinary gems, thanks to their excellent flavor and alluring scent. These mysterious fungus thrive beneath the soil of oak and hazelnut trees in the Dordogne, waiting to be discovered by professional truffle hunters and their canine partners.

Set out on a journey through the Dordogne's truffle-rich forests, where the air is filled with a beautiful earthy scent. Follow in the footsteps of truffle hunters as they navigate the terrain with precision and competence, their keen senses tuned to the hidden jewels beneath the surface. Witness the peace between man and dog as they labor together, the canine's nose guiding them to the precise locations where truffles are waiting to be uncovered.

Truffles are harvested and transported to vibrant local markets, where their arrival is met with anticipation and joy. Stroll among the crowded kiosks, taking in the exhibition of these gourmet treasures. Engage with the passionate merchants who are willing to share their knowledge and skills, providing insights into the characteristics, kinds, and best ways to enjoy truffles. From traditional truffle-infused dishes to inventive innovations, the Dordogne culinary world reveres and creatively embraces truffles, raising them to the stature of gastronomic royalty.

A trip to the Dordogne is an opportunity for foodies to sample the flavors of these renowned fungus. Allow yourself to be enchanted by the distinct earthy aroma and distinct umami flavor that truffles add to every dish. Enjoy truffle-infused omelets, creamy risottos, or tender slices of meat topped with subtle truffle shavings. Each bite is an invitation to savor the luxury and complexity that truffles provide, a true sensory thrill that stays long after the dinner is finished.

Truffles are more than just an ingredient in the Dordogne; they are a symbol of heritage, craftsmanship, and the region's deep relationship to the soil.

Foie Gras: A Delicacy to Savor

Prepare your taste buds for an unforgettable culinary experience as we explore the world of foie gras, a gastronomic masterpiece that symbolizes the essence of elegance and refinement. Foie gras has long been venerated in the culinary traditions of the Dordogne for its velvety texture and rich, buttery flavor. This delicacy, enjoyed by aficionados all over the world, is a monument to the region's dedication to the art of food.

The voyage begins with an investigation into the preparation of this exceptional delicacy. Foie gras is made from specially reared ducks or geese and translates to "fatty liver" in French. The birds are fed a carefully managed diet to stimulate the development of a rich, fatty liver, which is responsible for the delicacy's particular flavor and texture. Producing foie gras necessitates a precise balance of time, talent, and meticulous care to ensure the highest quality and flavor in every bite.

The Dordogne appreciates foie gras for reasons other than its great taste. It is a celebration of craftsmanship and tradition that have been passed down through the centuries. Visit local farms to see the delicate process of raising and caring for the birds. Engage with enthusiastic farmers who are dedicated to the time-honored practices that have made foie gras a lasting emblem of gastronomic excellence.

Savoring foie gras is a true sensory experience. The flavors dance on your palate as you savor a properly seared slice or a silky-smooth terrine, revealing layers of richness and depth. The delicate textural balance and beautiful blend of savory and gentle sweetness make for an enjoyable and unique experience. Combine it with a crisp glass of local wine for a flavor symphony that will take you to culinary pleasure.

Foie gras is a cultural icon in the Dordogne, a tribute to the region's passion for food and devotion to preserving culinary traditions. The predominance of foie gras on menus throughout the region, from Michelin-starred restaurants to rustic countryside pubs, demonstrates its importance in the local cuisine.

Bergerac and Bordeaux Wines: Toasting to Excellence

Welcome to the Dordogne, a wine lover's heaven where vines stretch as far as the eye can see and the art of winemaking has been elevated to a true craft. In this chapter, we raise our glasses to the region's great wines, with a particular emphasis on the renowned appellations of Bergerac and Bordeaux. Prepare to embark on a flavor and complexity journey as we explore the vineyards, meet passionate winemakers, and savor the liquid riches that have made the Dordogne an oenophilic delight.

The Dordogne's rolling hills and rich valleys provide the ideal environment for grape farming, resulting in wines of excellent quality and character. The Bergerac region, tucked along the banks of the Dordogne River, has a centuries-old viticultural legacy. Vineyards here create a wide range of wines, from crisp and refreshing whites to full-bodied reds and exquisite rosés. Explore the vineyards, where devoted winemakers use old and modern techniques to create wines that highlight the region's distinct terroir and microclimates.

We continue our journey into the world of wine, arriving in the world-renowned area of Bordeaux, only a stone's throw from the Dordogne. Bordeaux is linked with winemaking quality, and its famous reputation precedes it. The Bordeaux region is a tapestry of vineyards that create wines admired for their complexity and age-worthiness, from prestigious châteaux to family-run estates. Learn about the art of blending by watching winemakers expertly blend different grape varieties to achieve harmonious and diverse flavors. Each sip reveals the skill and accuracy that define Bordeaux wines, whether it's a silky Merlot, an elegant Cabernet Sauvignon, or a crisp Sauvignon Blanc.

Immerse yourself in the world of wine by visiting vineyards, tasting wines, and talking with the winemakers who put their heart and soul into their work. Learn about the diverse appellations, terroirs, and grape varietals that contribute to each bottle's unique tapestry of flavors. Every step of the winemaking process, from the vine to the cellar, is a labor of love, resulting in wines that encapsulate the essence of the Dordogne and its devotion to excellence.

CHAPTER 7:
IMMERSION IN LOCAL CULTURE

Immerse yourself in the colorful tapestry of Dordogne culture as we explore the region's heart and soul. This chapter allows you to explore the Dordogne's soul through its colorful markets, traditional festivals, and rich cultural past. The Dordogne provides a rich and compelling cultural experience, from lively marketplaces that tempt your senses to captivating celebrations of heritage and craftsmanship.

Step into the vibrant markets that dot the Dordogne's towns and villages, where an abundance of sights, sounds, and fragrances will stimulate your senses. Participate in conversations with local artisans and farmers as they proudly display their produce, crafts, and gastronomic pleasures. Taste the region's wealth, which includes everything from ripe fruits and vegetables to artisanal cheeses, freshly baked bread, and delectable pastries. These markets not only allow you to sample the delicacies of the Dordogne, but they also provide you with a look into the lives of its locals, generating a sense of connection and community.

As you immerse yourself in the local culture, you'll have the opportunity to participate in traditional festivities that bring age-old customs and traditions to life. Witness the Dordogne's lively energy and infectious enthusiasm as villagers gather to celebrate their heritage via music, dance, and colorful processions. From the jubilant celebrations of Bastille Day to the mesmerizing spectacle of medieval reenactments, these events provide a glimpse into the region's rich history and cultural identity.

The Dordogne is also a refuge for artists and craftspeople who have perfected their abilities over centuries. Explore the countryside's workshops and studios, where skilled artisans bring their creations to life. The Dordogne's cultural tradition is vast, ranging from pottery and porcelain to woodworking, painting, and delicate lacework. Engage with these creative individuals, learn about their skills, and possibly take home a one-of-a-kind piece of the Dordogne's artistic legacy.

Vibrant Markets: A Feast for the Senses

Immerse yourself in the colorful and beautiful ambience of the Dordogne's towns and villages' thriving markets. These markets are more than just places to shop; they are hives of activity, bringing the region's rich agricultural past to life. The sights, sounds, and fragrances that pervade the air will stimulate your senses as you walk through the colorful stalls.

The Dordogne markets offer a feast for the senses, tempting you with a variety of fresh fruit, local specialties, and artisanal crafts. Enjoy the colorful array of fruits and vegetables that mirror the changing seasons, each one brimming with flavor and vitality. Taste the artisanal cheeses, cured meats, and aromatic spices that highlight the region's culinary prowess. Indulge in the freshly baked bread and pastries that entice you with their delectable fragrances. These markets are a culinary treasure trove, allowing you to immerse yourself in the Dordogne's flavors and customs.

Aside from the delectable array of food, the markets offer an opportunity to interact with the local population and see the rhythm of daily life. Interact with passionate farmers and producers who are proud of their offerings, giving tales and recommendations that capture the character of the place. You'll find unique crafts and handmade goods that highlight the beauty and craftsmanship of the Dordogne as you browse the stalls. These markets are a refuge for anyone looking for unique and locally crafted goods, with everything from handwoven fabrics and detailed pottery to beautiful jewelry and decorative objects.

Immerse yourself in the Dordogne's bustling markets, where the beauty of the region's agricultural bounty meets the kindness of its people. Allow the sights, sounds, and flavors to captivate your senses as you explore these buzzing cultural hotspots. Whether you're a foodie, a curious visitor, or an avid shopper, the Dordogne markets provide an amazing experience, allowing you to taste, discover, and connect with the heart and soul of this wonderful region.

Traditional Festivals: Celebrating Heritage and Tradition

As we explore the Dordogne's traditional festivals, we will enter a world of lively customs and joyful celebrations. These vibrant and colorful events offer a glimpse into the region's rich cultural heritage and deep-rooted customs. The Dordogne festivals are a true celebration of life and community, with everything from music and dancing to elaborate processions and age-old rituals.

The Dordogne comes alive with a plethora of events that celebrate various parts of local culture throughout the year. There is always a reason to rejoice in the Dordogne, from religious processions that pay homage to centuries-old traditions to colorful street festivals that bring together locals and visitors alike. The infectious enthusiasm of events such as the Fête de la Musique, where the streets are filled with the sounds of live music, or the Fête des Fleurs, a vivid floral celebration that transforms cities into fragrant havens of beauty, is also worth experiencing.

These events will showcase the talent and passion of local artists through engaging performances of traditional music and dance, elaborate costumes, energetic rhythms, and elaborate choreography that will take you to another time and place. Participate in the festivities as the streets come alive with laughter, music, and the Dordogne's joyous energy.

These traditional events also provide an opportunity to sample the culinary delicacies of the region. From street food booths providing delightful sweets to communal feasts highlighting Dordogne's gastronomic legacy, you'll have the opportunity to sample the flavors of the region while immersing yourself in its vivid festivals. Traditional foods such as confit de canard, truffle-infused delights, and regional specialties passed down through generations are available.

The Dordogne's traditional festivals provide an insight into the region's character, where legacy and tradition are honored with zeal and delight. Participate in these colorful and intriguing events to immerse yourself in the lively atmosphere.

Art and Craftsmanship: Discovering Local Talents

Explore the Dordogne's rich creative legacy and immerse yourself in the enchanting world of art and craftsmanship. This lovely region is known not only for its breathtaking surroundings but also for its plethora of skilled artists and craftspeople. The Dordogne is a treasure trove of talent waiting to be explored, with everything from pottery and painting to woodworking and lacework.

You'll come across workshops and studios where local artisans bring their thoughts to life as you travel through the picturesque villages and cities. Step inside these creative locations to witness directly the skill of their profession. Admire the delicate details of handcrafted pottery, with each piece conveying a different story through its design and finish. Admire the painters' deft brushstrokes as they capture the essence of the Dordogne's beauty on canvas. Discover the realm of woodworking, where experienced artisans turn raw materials into stunning furniture and ornamental things. Discover the delicate craft of lacework as workers weave beautiful patterns that reflect the region's rich textile legacy.

Engaging with these gifted individuals provides a once-in-a-lifetime opportunity to learn about their approaches, inspirations, and the stories behind their works. Many Dordogne artists are profoundly connected to their surroundings, deriving inspiration from the stunning scenery, attractive villages, and ever-changing light play. They find beauty in the mundane and transform it into spectacular works of art.

Aside from the workshops, Dordogne has a thriving art culture, with galleries and shows showcasing the region's unique skills. From modern art to traditional crafts, the Dordogne offers a diverse range of artistic expressions that reflect the dynamic essence of creation. Explore these locations and become immersed in the artistic debate that thrives in the region.

CHAPTER 8:
7-DAY ITINERARY IN DORDOGNE

Day 1: Arrival and Exploring Sarlat-la-Canéda

Morning:

Welcome to the wonderful Dordogne region! You will be met by the splendor of the countryside as you make your way to your accommodation after arriving at the specified airport or train station. Take in the scenery and breathe in the fresh air, allowing the excitement of your Dordogne trip to build.

Afternoon:

After you've settled into your accommodation, it's time to start exploring the area. Begin your tour in the heart of Dordogne, where you may immerse yourself in the historic beauty of Sarlat-la-mayéda. With its tiny cobblestone alleys, well-preserved architecture, and rich history, this charming village is a wonderful voyage through time.

Stroll around the bustling market squares, where local traders proudly display their fresh fruit, handcrafted goods, and tempting delicacies. Immerse yourself in the dynamic ambiance while sampling regional dishes and indulging in Sarlat-la-Canéda's gourmet delights. Take a moment to enjoy the spectacular medieval structures, such as the Cathédrale Saint-Sacerdos and the Maison de la Boétie, and the fine features that transport you back in time.

Evening:
Find a nice restaurant in the heart of Sarlat-la-Canéda as the sun begins to set and treat yourself to a fantastic dining experience. Savor the flavors of the region by indulging in regional specialties such as foie gras, truffles, and the world-famous Bergerac and Bordeaux wines. Allow the town's ambiance to mesmerize you as you enjoy a leisurely evening eating gastronomic delicacies and meditating on the day's glories.

Accommodation:
Return to your lovely Sarlat-la-Canéda accommodation after a day of discovery and enjoyment. Whether you choose a quaint bed and breakfast, a quiet boutique hotel, or a

rustic countryside retreat, you will wake up refreshed and ready for the experiences that await you in the days ahead.

Day 2: Exploring Beynac-et-Cazenac and the Dordogne River

Morning:
Wake up to the tranquil beauty of the Dordogne countryside and fill up with a hearty meal at your lodging. Today, you'll go to the enchanting village of Beynac-et-Cazenac, where history comes to life.

Take a lovely trip over the winding lanes that lead to this medieval wonder. The majestic Château de Beynac, built high on a rock overlooking the Dordogne River, will greet you as you enter the settlement. Discover the picturesque alleyways dotted with old stone cottages and the wonderful ambience that has enchanted travelers for generations.

Climb to the château and learn about its fascinating history. Explore its majestic halls, ascend the spiral staircases, and take in the breathtaking views from the summit. Learn about the noble families that once lived in this stronghold and envision the stories that took place behind its walls.

Afternoon:
As the sun sets, head to the banks of the Dordogne River for a pleasant afternoon activity: a leisurely canoe journey. Glide through the calm waterways, surrounded by rich flora and the region's stunning scenery. Enjoy the tranquility of the river as you paddle at your own speed, taking in the scenery.

Take stops along the journey to see the natural marvels and maybe even stop for a picnic by the river. Allow yourself to be immersed in the tranquility of the Dordogne River, reconnecting with nature and enjoying the solitude that only a river vacation can offer.

Evening:
Return to Beynac-et-Cazenac at the end of the day and choose a nice restaurant for a delicious dinner. Indulge in regional flavors by eating local cuisine cooked with fresh ingredients gathered from the Dordogne's lush soil. Raise a glass of local wine and salute the day's events, celebrating

the beauty and history that you've had the opportunity to see.

Day 3: Discovering the Prehistoric Wonders of the Vézère Valley

Morning:
Rise and shine for another exciting day in the Dordogne. Today, you'll explore the prehistoric treasures of the Vézère Valley, a time portal to the past. After a hearty breakfast, depart for your first destination: the world-famous Lascaux caves.

Prepare to be amazed by the ancient cave art that stretches back thousands of years as you visit the Lascaux Cave Complex. Explore the famous Lascaux II replica, which closely recreates the original cave paintings discovered in 1940. Admire the complex sketches and paintings that show prehistoric life, providing an insight into our ancient ancestors' artistic prowess and cultural heritage.

Afternoon:

Visit the Font-de-Gaume Cave to continue your exploration of the Vézère Valley. This cave is famous for its well-preserved polychrome paintings and provides a completely immersive insight into prehistoric life. Venture deep inside the cave with an experienced guide to see the incredible artwork covering its walls. Admire the vibrant colors and meticulous attention to detail, and allow the stories depicted in these ancient masterpieces to transport you back in time.

As the day continues, head to the Rouffignac Cave, commonly known as the "Cave of Hundred Mammoths," and board a tiny train that will transport you deep into the heart of this amazing cave. The walls are adorned with amazing engravings and drawings of mammoths, horses, and other Ice Age animals. It's an enthralling experience that gives you a glimpse into the lives of our ancient forefathers and the animals they coexisted with.

Evening:

After a day of exploring prehistoric wonders, return to your lodging and take some time to rest and reflect on your fantastic findings. Enjoy a relaxing evening by taking a stroll through the beautiful streets of a local village, eating a good meal, or simply relaxing in the tranquil surroundings of the Dordogne.

Day 4: Immersing in Natural Beauty - Gardens and Grotto Exploration

Morning:

Wake up to the sun's soft rays illuminating the Dordogne landscape. Today, you'll immerse yourself in the region's natural splendor, beginning with a visit to the stunning gardens of Marqueyssac.

Marqueyssac Gardens, located in the heart of the Périgord Noir, is a fascinating exhibition of perfectly groomed hedges, twisting walks, and breathtaking panoramic views. Take a leisurely stroll through the gorgeous gardens, inhaling the aroma of vivid flowers and listening to nature's soothing noises. Discover secret nooks, lovely gazebos, and wonderfully positioned vistas that showcase the splendor of the Dordogne Valley as you lose yourself in the tranquility of the surroundings.

Afternoon:

Continue your natural wonder journey by visiting the Gouffre de Proumeyssac, also known as the "Crystal Cathedral." Enter the massive underground cave and marvel at the awe-inspiring formations of stalactites and stalagmites that sparkle like crystals. Take a guided tour that will take you deep into the heart of this geological wonder, exposing the secrets of its formation as well as the interesting stories it carries. The play of light and shadow, as well as the fascinating reflections in the underground lake, will captivate you.

As the day continues, make your way to Les Jardins de l'Imaginaire in Terrasson-Lavilledieu, a lovely town. These remarkable gardens are a true aesthetic masterpiece, combining breathtaking landscapes with cutting-edge art pieces. Discover the meticulously constructed pathways, cascading water features, and carefully tended vegetation that create a natural and artistic symphony. Take your time admiring the well-constructed areas that promote reflection and excite the imagination.

Evening:

Find a nice restaurant tucked away in the Dordogne countryside as the sun begins to set and treat yourself to a delicious dinner. Indulge in the pleasures of the region, experiencing fresh local food and culinary delights that highlight Dordogne's gastronomic brilliance. Raise a glass of local wine to the beauty of nature and the day's amazing adventures.

Day 5: Visiting Historic Towns and Villages

Morning:

Awaken to a spirit of adventure as you set out to discover the medieval cities and villages of the Dordogne. After a hearty breakfast, travel to Sarlat-la-Canéda, a lovely village famed for its well-preserved medieval buildings and charming small alleyways. Wander through the ancient district, admiring the golden sandstone structures and taking in the lovely ambience. Discover the vibrant market square, where local sellers sell fresh produce, artisanal crafts, and scrumptious regional delicacies.

Afternoon:

Visit the charming village of Beynac-et-Cazenac to continue your exploration of the region's rich history. Be intrigued as you approach the village by the towering silhouette of the Château de Beynac located atop a steep cliff. Take a stroll around the picturesque streets packed with historic homes, small stores, and pleasant cafes. Immerse yourself in the medieval atmosphere and learn about the interesting stories that reverberate through the cobblestone pathways. Climb to the château for panoramic views of the Dordogne River and surrounding landscape if you're up for it.

Evening:

As the day fades into twilight, make your way to Domme, a village located high above the Dordogne. This bastide town has stunning views of the river valley and verdant landscape. Take a leisurely stroll along the fortress walls, taking in the panoramic views that spread before you. Discover the lovely streets lined with flower-filled balconies and antique structures. Savor the delicacies of the region while basking in the wonderful ambience of this hilltop village with a superb dinner at one of the local eateries.

Day 6: Prehistoric Treasures and Local Delights

Morning:

Begin your day with a visit to the legendary Lascaux IV, a replica of the famous Lascaux Cave. Explore the intricate paintings that represent ancient life as you enter the immersive world of prehistoric art. As you learn about the significance and purpose behind these extraordinary artworks, marvel at our forefathers' accuracy and craftsmanship. Explore the Paleolithic era's mysteries to obtain a better understanding of the early human civilizations that once inhabited the Dordogne region.

Afternoon:

Continue your exploration of the Dordogne's prehistoric wonders by visiting the interesting National Museum of Prehistory in Les Eyzies-de-Tayac. Explore a wide collection of artifacts, tools, and archaeological finds that illuminate the region's rich prehistoric legacy. Learn about the Neanderthals and early Homo sapiens who lived in these areas thousands of years ago. Explore the interactive displays and participate in hands-on activities that provide visitors of all ages with a unique and informative experience.

Take a break from the ancient past as the afternoon passes and enjoy a delectable culinary experience. Make your way to a local farm or restaurant to sample the world-renowned foie gras, a Dordogne specialty. Learn about its traditional production processes and savor its rich and distinct flavor. Pair it with a glass of Bergerac or Bordeaux wine, both of which are known for their superb quality and tastes that perfectly suit the local cuisine.

Evening:
Take a leisurely stroll around the picturesque streets of a local village or town, such as Sarlat-la-Canéda or Bergerac, as the sun sets. Explore the local stores, boutiques, and artisanal workshops to immerse yourself in the pleasant ambiance and colorful atmosphere. Discover one-of-a-kind souvenirs, handcrafted goods, and locally produced goods that highlight the region's artistic talents and traditional craftsmanship. Finish the day with a fantastic dinner at a local restaurant, where you may experience the flavors of the Dordogne one last time.

Day 7: Farewell to Dordogne

Morning:
Take a leisurely morning on your final day in the Dordogne to absorb the quiet beauty of the countryside. Enjoy a leisurely breakfast while savoring the flavors of fresh-baked pastries and local fruit. As you bid farewell to the accommodations, take a moment to reflect on the memories you've made throughout your time in this enthralling region.

After that, travel to the lovely village of Rocamadour, which is set high on a cliffside. Explore the old pilgrimage site, complete with small alleyways, ancient structures, and stunning views of the surrounding valleys. Visit the famed Rocamadour Sanctuary, a significant religious place that draws visitors from all over the world. Take a peaceful stroll down the Grand Escalier, a massive stairway leading to the sanctuaries, and stop to observe the beautiful carvings and stunning architecture.

Afternoon:

As the day continues, head out into the beautiful Dordogne countryside for a tranquil and scenic lunch. Find a beautiful location by a river or in a shaded grove, surrounded by nature's magnificence. Unwrap a basket full of delectable local treats, artisanal cheeses, freshly baked bread, and seasonal fruits. Take your time, savoring the flavors and taking in the tranquility of your surroundings. Consider the great experiences and discoveries you've had while traveling around the Dordogne.

Evening:

Return to your accommodation or locate a warm area in one of the picturesque villages as the sun begins to set to experience the stunning hues of the Dordogne's sunset. Relax and think about the adventures you've had, the sites you've seen, and the memories you've formed. Enjoy a farewell evening at a local restaurant, relishing regional specialties and raising a glass to honor the extraordinary adventure you've had in the Dordogne.

CHAPTER 9: PRACTICAL INFORMATION AND TIPS

Etiquette and Customs

When visiting the Dordogne region, it is important to become acquainted with the local etiquette and customs in order to have a polite and pleasurable experience. Here are some helpful tips to remember:

Greetings and Politeness: The French place a high priority on politeness, and greetings are essential. It is traditional to greet the workers with a friendly "Bonjour" (Good day) or "Bonsoir" (Good evening), depending on the time of day. When getting assistance or service, saying "Merci" (Thank you) is also appreciated.

Dress Code: While the Dordogne has a relaxed atmosphere, it's advisable to dress modestly while visiting churches, religious sites, or luxury places. Respect for cultural and religious traditions calls for modest clothing that covers the shoulders and knees.

Meal Etiquette: It is traditional to wait to be seated at a restaurant rather than choosing a table yourself. Remember that the French take their time savoring their meals, so be patient and enjoy the gourmet experience. It is customary to use utensils when eating and to place your hands on the table rather than on your lap.

Language: Because French is the region's official language, learning a few simple words might help you communicate with the residents. While many people speak English in tourist areas, making an effort to greet and order in French would be appreciated.

Tipping: It is traditional to leave a small tip of 5-10% of the total bill in restaurants, even if service costs are sometimes included. You can either give the server the tip or leave it on the table when you depart. It is also standard practice to round up the amount or leave tiny change for services such as taxi trips or hotel workers.

Shop Hours: The Dordogne adheres to traditional French shop hours, with many shops closing for a few hours in the afternoon. Plan your shopping ahead of time, and keep in mind that some smaller businesses and restaurants may be closed on Sundays or Mondays.

Respect for Heritage Sites: When visiting historical places, abide by the norms and guidelines that have been established. Some places may have photographic limitations or specific areas that are off-limits. It is important to follow these rules in order to preserve the region's cultural history.

By following local customs and etiquette, you will enjoy a more immersive and respectful experience in the Dordogne. Remember to be friendly and open-minded and to enjoy the fascinating region's unique cultural traditions.

Language and Communication

When visiting the Dordogne region, language and communication skills are essential. Here are some useful tips that will help you overcome language difficulties and improve your communication during your stay:

French Language: While many people in tourist destinations speak English, it is always useful to acquire a few basic French phrases. Greetings such as "Bonjour" (Hello), "Merci" (Thank you), and "Au revoir" (Goodbye) can go a long way toward establishing rapport and showing respect to the locals.

Phrasebook or Language App: Carry a phrasebook or install a language app on your mobile device. These tools can help you communicate in a variety of scenarios, such as ordering food, asking for directions, or shopping.

Etiquette and Politeness: In French society, politeness is highly valued. When talking with locals, use "s'il vous plaît" (please) and "merci" (thank you). It is considered respectful to begin conversations with a polite greeting and to use formal pronouns ("vous") rather than casual ones ("tu") when addressing strangers or older folks.

Nonverbal Communication: Nonverbal cues can express meaning and intention as well. Maintain eye contact when communicating with someone, smile, and use appropriate gestures to improve understanding. However, keep in mind that gestures might have different meanings in different cultures, so pay attention and adjust accordingly.

Language Assistance: If you're having trouble communicating in French, don't be afraid to ask for help. Even if they don't speak English well, locals are usually pleasant and willing to help. To convey your message, you can use simple English phrases, point to maps or signs, or use visual aids.

Patience and Understanding: Language limitations can occasionally lead to misconceptions or miscommunications. Maintain patience, remain open-minded, and approach circumstances with understanding and flexibility. Remember that the locals will appreciate you learning a few important phrases and making an attempt to converse in French.

Translators and Language Services: Consider hiring expert translators or language services if you need more in-depth assistance or need to engage in critical conversations. These sites can provide reliable translations and improve communication in difficult situations.

By embracing the French language and culture, as well as using these communication guidelines, you can improve your relationships and create unforgettable encounters during your stay in the Dordogne. The locals will appreciate your efforts, and your journey will be more immersive and pleasurable.

Simple French Phrases to Know

Here are some simple French phrases in many categories that you could find useful during your stay in the Dordogne:

Greetings and Basic Phrases:
Bonjour - Hello
Bonsoir - Good evening
Au revoir - Goodbye
Merci - Thank you
S'il vous plaît - Please
Excusez-moi - Excuse me
Pardon - Sorry

Getting Around:
Où est... ? - Where is...?
Je cherche... - I'm looking for...
À gauche - To the left
À droite - To the right
Tout droit - Straight ahead
Combien ça coûte ? - How much does it cost?
Un billet, s'il vous plaît - One ticket, please
Parlez-vous anglais ? - Do you speak English?

Dining and Food:

Une table pour deux, s'il vous plaît - A table for two, please

Je voudrais... - I would like...

L'addition, s'il vous plaît - The bill, please

Une bouteille d'eau - A bottle of water

Qu'est-ce que vous recommandez ? - What do you recommend?

Délicieux - Delicious

L'addition est comprise ? - Is the tip included?

Shopping:

Combien ça coûte ? - How much does it cost?

Je voudrais l'essayer - I would like to try it on

C'est trop cher - It's too expensive

Je peux payer par carte ? - Can I pay by card?

Avez-vous un plus grand/plus petit ? - Do you have a larger/smaller one?

Est-ce que vous pouvez l'emballer, s'il vous plaît ? - Can you wrap it, please?

Emergencies:

Au secours ! - Help!

Je ne me sens pas bien - I don't feel well

Où est l'hôpital le plus proche ? - Where is the nearest hospital?

J'ai perdu mon passeport - I lost my passport

Appelez la police - Call the police

These phrases might help you communicate and manage various circumstances during your stay in the Dordogne. Remember to practice and be patient, and the locals will appreciate your efforts.

Health and Safety Tips

When visiting the Dordogne, it is critical to prioritize your health and safety in order to have a pleasant and memorable time. Here are a few health and safety reminders:

Travel Insurance: Make sure you have travel insurance that covers medical bills and emergencies before you leave. This will give you peace of mind and financial security in the event of an unanticipated event.

Vaccinations: Consult your doctor or a travel clinic to check if any vaccinations are required for your trip to the Dordogne. It is critical to stay current on routine vaccines and to consider additional ones based on your individual travel intentions.

Medications and Prescriptions: If you require prescription medications, be sure you have enough for the duration of your trip. Carry them in their original packaging, and bring a copy of your prescriptions with you. It's also a good idea to look into neighboring pharmacies in case you need to refill or buy drugs.

Hygiene and Food Safety: Maintain proper hygiene by washing your hands with soap and water on a frequent basis, especially before meals. Choose restaurants with appropriate sanitary measures and cooked items that are served hot when dining out. If the tap water is unsafe to drink, drink bottled water or use a water filter.

Sun protection: During the summer, the Dordogne region experiences sunny weather. Wear sunscreen with a high SPF, a hat, and sunglasses to protect yourself from the sun's damaging rays. To avoid heat-related diseases, stay hydrated and seek shade during the warmest parts of the day.

Outdoor Safety: If you intend to participate in outdoor activities such as hiking or exploring natural locations, become familiar with the trails, routes, and safety requirements. Dress appropriately, wear sturdy shoes, and bring any essential equipment, such as maps, compasses, and first aid kits. Keep an eye on your surroundings and heed any cautions or instructions.

Emergency Services: Save emergency contact information on your phone and become acquainted with your local emergency services. Contact the relevant authorities for assistance in the event of a medical emergency, accident, or incident.

Personal Belongings: Always keep your personal belongings secure, especially in crowded settings or tourist regions. Carry large sums of cash and valuable objects only when absolutely required. Keep your passports, extra cash, and other vital documents in hotel safes or secure lockers.

By following these health and safety precautions, you can reduce hazards and have a safe and enjoyable visit to the Dordogne. Remember to stay alert and be aware of your surroundings, and seek help or guidance when necessary.

Emergency Contacts

Here are some key contact numbers in case of an emergency during your vacation to the Dordogne:

Police Emergency: 17

In the event of an immediate threat to your safety, a criminal occurrence, or the need for police help, phone this number.

Medical Emergency: 15

In the event of a medical emergency, an accident, or the need for an ambulance, dial this number. The operator will put you in touch with the necessary medical services.

Fire Department: 18

In the event of a fire or other emergency, dial this number to contact the local fire department.

European Emergency Number: 112

This is a toll-free line that may be reached from anywhere in the European Union, including the Dordogne. Based on your location, it will connect you to the appropriate emergency services.

It is important to keep these emergency numbers close at hand and easily accessible. Save them on your phone or write them down somewhere you can easily refer to them if necessary. Inform your trip companions of these contact numbers as well, so that everyone is prepared in case of an emergency.

Please keep in mind that emergency services may have varied response times and capabilities in your home country. Travel insurance that covers emergency medical treatment and repatriation is always recommended, as is keeping critical documents and contact information in a secure location.

Communication and Internet Access

Here are some important things to remember about communication and internet access in the Dordogne:

Language: French is the official language of France, including the Dordogne region. While English is widely spoken and understood in tourist regions, learning a few basic French words will help you communicate with locals. They will value your efforts to communicate in their language.

Mobile Network Coverage: The Dordogne has excellent mobile network coverage, particularly in urban regions and important tourist sites. Orange, SFR, Bouygues Telecom, and Free Mobile are the major mobile network operators in France. Before your vacation, inquire with your service provider about foreign roaming plans and pricing.

SIM Cards: If you want a local phone number and mobile data access during your stay, you can buy a prepaid SIM card from one of the local mobile network carriers. This allows you to make cheaper local calls, send text messages, and access mobile data. Assure that your phone is unlocked and compatible with the GSM network in France.

Wi-Fi Availability: Wi-Fi is frequently provided in hotels, cafes, restaurants, and public locations across the Dordogne. Many hotels provide free Wi-Fi to their visitors, and internet cafes and public libraries are also available. Some tourist attractions and visitor centers may offer free Wi-Fi as well.

Internet Access in Rural Areas: While urban regions have consistent internet connection, rural locations in the Dordogne may have limited coverage or slower internet speeds. Be prepared for internet connectivity issues if you want to visit remote places.

Offline Maps and Translation Apps: Download offline maps or utilize map apps before your journey to access maps and navigation without an internet connection. Consider installing translation applications to help you communicate and understand simple phrases, even if you don't have internet access.

Internet Cafes and Libraries: If you need internet access for extended periods of time or have certain tasks to do, you can go to internet cafes or public libraries that charge a fee for computer and internet services.

To minimize surprise fees, check with your mobile service provider regarding overseas data roaming charges. It's also a good idea to have a backup plan for communication, such as carrying a physical map or writing down vital contact numbers in case of internet or phone service outages.

Useful Apps, Websites, and Maps

There are various handy applications, websites, and maps that enhance your trip experience in the Dordogne. Here are a few suggestions:

Google Maps: This well-known mapping app is ideal for traversing the Dordogne. You may look up specific destinations, obtain directions, and even use offline maps if you download them ahead of time. It also includes information on neighboring attractions, restaurants, and lodging.

TripAdvisor: The TripAdvisor app is an excellent resource for getting recommendations and reviews about Dordogne hotels, restaurants, and sights. Based on the experiences of other visitors, it can help you make informed selections about where to stay, eat, and see.

Visit Dordogne's Official Website: The Dordogne Tourism Board's official website (www.visitdordogne.com) gives detailed information about the region's attractions, events, lodgings, and activities. It also provides suggested itineraries and useful travel advice.

Michelin Green Guide: The Michelin Green Guide gives thorough information about the Dordogne's cultural and ecological attractions. It provides detailed descriptions, maps, and ratings to assist you in planning your visits and exploring the region's highlights.

XE Currency: If you're coming from another currency zone, the XE Currency app can help you convert currencies and track exchange rates. It allows you to rapidly compute pricing and expenses in the currency of your choice.

French-English Dictionary App: Having language translation software can help you communicate with locals or comprehend signs and menus. Apps such as "Google Translate" and "Linguee" offer translations and even voice recognition to help you overcome language barriers.

Dordogne Tourist Guide: Several smartphone applications, like "Dordogne Tourist Guide," are specifically intended for touring the Dordogne and include information about local sites, hiking trails, cultural events, and practical suggestions for visitors.

Additionally, check the websites or download the applications of specific attractions or activities you intend to visit, as many museums, châteaux, and outdoor sites have their own dedicated apps or online resources.

You can easily obtain information, plan your itinerary, and make the most of your stay in the Dordogne by using these apps, websites, and maps. To avoid connectivity troubles when traveling, download offline maps or use Wi-Fi when available.

CONCLUSION

As we come to the end of this Dordogne Travel Guide, it's evident that this region of France has something to offer every traveler. Dordogne has something for everyone, from its rich history and medieval villages to prehistoric treasures, imposing châteaux, outdoor experiences, gastronomy, and absorption in local culture.

We've gone through useful information on when to travel, how to get there, how to get around, where to stay, and what to bring, which makes planning your trip to Dordogne easier. Understanding local customs and language, as well as having emergency contacts on hand, will ensure a pleasant and safe voyage.

We have explored the distinctive attractions, hidden jewels, and must-see sites that make Dordogne a great destination throughout this book. With their cobblestone alleys, ancient architecture, and pleasant ambience, the medieval villages of the region, such as Sarlat-la-Canéda, Beynac-et-Cazenac, and Domme, transport you back in time.

Dordogne châteaux, such as Castelnaud, Beynac, and Hautefort, ooze grandeur and history, transporting you to the region's feudal past. The prehistoric wonders of the Vézère Valley, such as Lascaux, Font-de-Gaume, and Rouffignac, provide a fascinating view into the creative and cultural achievements of our ancient predecessors.

Dordogne's tranquil river getaways, attractive hiking routes, and magnificent hot air balloon tours give amazing natural experiences for adventure enthusiasts. The region's food tantalizes the taste buds and honors the region's gastronomic heritage, with truffles, foie gras, and renowned Bergerac and Bordeaux wines.

Immersion in local culture through colorful markets, traditional festivals, and exploration of Dordogne art and craftsmanship shows the region's real personality and provides a greater appreciation of its origins.

Dordogne welcomes you to go on a magnificent adventure filled with amazing moments, whether you are a history buff, nature lover, food aficionado, or cultural traveler.

Dordogne catches the heart and creates a lasting impact, from its breathtaking landscapes to its friendliness.

So, start planning your trip to Dordogne today and immerse yourself in the enchantment of this magnificent region. Allow it to transport you to a world of timeless beauty and enchantment with its medieval villages, ancient caves, grand châteaux, and superb food. Dordogne's delights await your exploration. Best wishes!